Savoy

Eugene O'Brien

Methuen Drama

Published by Methuen Drama 2004

1 3 5 7 9 10 8 6 4 2

First published in 2004 by
Methuen Drama
Bloomsbury Publishing Plc
50 Bedford Square
London WC1B 3DP
www.methuendrama.com

Copyright © 2004 by Eugene O'Brien

Eugene O'Brien has asserted his rights under the Copyright, Designs
and Patents Act, 1988, to be identified as the author of this work

A CIP catalogue record for this book is available from the British Library

ISBN 978 0 4137 7440 8

Typeset by Country Setting, Kingsdown, Kent

Savoy

By Eugene O'Brien

The Abbey Theatre gratefully acknowledges the financial support
from the Arts Council/an Chomhairle Ealaíon

New Writing Centre Stage

The Abbey Theatre was founded to develop and promote a canon of Irish dramatic literature, and from Yeats, Synge, O'Casey through to the writers of the modern period it has held faith with that mission. Over seven hundred new works have premiered on our stages in the past one hundred years so it is entirely appropriate that **The Abbey and New Writing** should be a pervasive strand of our five-pronged programme for **abbey**onehundred.

In selecting these works for presentation in this special year Ali Curran, the Director of the Peacock, and I were mindful of the need to show the scope and breadth of new writing for the Irish stage. Hence in this season we are presenting storytelling theatre from Paula Meehan, **The Wolf of Winter**, particularly for children and families; Peter Sheridan's **Finders Keepers**, set in the heart of 1960's Dublin; the drama of contemporary Ireland in **Savoy** and **Defender of the Faith** by two young and very talented writers, Eugene O' Brien and Stuart Carolan, and **Smokescreen**, a challenging work from one of the most iconoclastic writer/directors of this or any other generation, Paul Mercier.

With this season we re-affirm the centrality of new writing to the Abbey project and invite you to enjoy and to support the lifeblood of this theatre, **New Writing at the Abbey**.

Ben Barnes
Artistic Director

CINEMA PURGATORIO

There was no cinema in our local town in Leitrim. But every now and again films were shown on a small screen in the secondary school. Westerns mainly. In or around the mid seventies *Some Like It Hot* was shown as part of a summer festival. And a very holy woman went on the rampage denouncing foreign filth and all who sat to watch it. I think she even made a placard. The audience loved the film. Nobody is perfect.

A town didn't need a cinema to have its own dramas: the watchers watching; the actors playing their daily part, brilliant, duplicitous... Daily walkabouts worthy of an Oscar, up and down the street, in and out of shops and bars and rooms. Low noon and lower midnight. Dreams long soured and abandoned. Hopes gone west or east or just stalled and rusted and locked inside. No cinema, but the telly in every pub, in every house; the soaps *('shite people watch with their tea')* a handy distraction from life, something to talk about, to ward off too much reality.

The biggest small town (Carrick-on-Shannon) had its cinema: I polished my shoes at the age of eight to see my first film there, *The Bridge on the River Kwai*; and in my teens spent many happy weekend nights in the Gaiety, watching the world and Dustin Hoffman. Those early screen experiences were much more than entertainment or distraction: they laid down a strong sense of the visual, a sense of what might be achieved in life. And, of course, there was the occasional *coort* to sweeten the hours.

The cinema: a place where myth and fantasy and colour whirled out of the darkness and reigned for a brief time. Where lust was allowed or possible or imaginable. Where you could escape for a while – if not under a skirt, then into the light of other places, other times, meeting characters who might be you or a little of what you might be. A healthy alternative to church and pub. Cheaper than drink, freer than enforced worship.

Eugene O'Brien's *Savoy* is no Cinema Paradiso. More Purgatorio. Where characters rehearse and play endless versions of their lives. Like the worlds created by Billy Roche and Tom Murphy, O'Brien's small town is rich in language, in loss and in the grudging, edgy exchange of everyday lies and truth. Disillusion and regret hover behind cocky bravado; bitterness tinges life like invisible rust; memory is suppressed, making occasional, desperate signals for attention out of a swilling flood of alcohol. Yet a small, thwarted glimmer of human need and near-compassion throws its dusty ray over Andy and David and Pax, and if everything goes on as before, profound change has also taken place. For once, the film has been shown in full, with all the out takes, and with the ending that was tried out on a test audience and judged too harsh, too real. Bring on the candles flickering as the crowd gathers outside to bid a tearful farewell to their beloved cinema... Maybe even save it from the wrecking ball. Yeah. And Fellini was a Dutch Lutheran.

Small town Ireland is an animal all of its own: The Mouse, The Badger, The Body find their home there and won't make sentimental gestures for anyone (except maybe their mother when she's dead). There's a kind of innocence in and around the Savoy, a deadly kind; how many secret, desperate lifelines... Now there's the Net to deal with - but that's another play, another day. Another Fistful of Dollars.

Vincent Woods

Vincent Woods, poet and playwright. His last collection of poems, *Lives And Miracles*, (Arlen House) won the Ted McNulty poetry award. He is writing a new version of *Deirdre* for the Abbey Theatre.

Savoy

By Eugene O'Brien

Savoy by Eugene O'Brien was first performed at the Peacock Theatre, Dublin on 5th May 2004. Press night was 10th May 2004.

The play is set in The Savoy Cinema, Edenderry in 1994.

There will be one interval of 15 minutes.

Cast

David	Fergal McElherron
Andy	Jim Norton
Pax	John Olohan
Podge	Steve Blount
Liz	Karen Scully

Director	Conall Morrison
Designer	Bláithín Sheerin
Lighting Designer	Ian Scott
Sound	Eddie Breslin
Voice Director	Andrea Ainsworth
Stage Director	Audrey Hession
Assistant Stage Manager	Marguerita Corscadden
Casting Director	Marie Kelly
Dramaturg	Jocelyn Clarke
Set	Abbey Theatre Workshop
Costumes	Abbey Theatre Wardrobe Department
Photography	Tom Lawlor
Publicity	Gerry Lundberg PR

Eugene O'Brien *Author*

Eugene wrote and performed monologues **America '87** and **Checking for Squirrels**. He co-wrote the short films **Cold Turkey** and **America A Movie** and wrote **The Nest** for RTE Radio. He wrote **Solid** which was part of The Corn Exchange's **Car Show** and **Ten** for Semper Fi. Eugene's first full-length play **Eden** premiered at the Peacock Theatre in January 2001, played at the Abbey Theatre in December 2001 and transferred to the Arts Theatre, London in October 2002 before returning to the Peacock in March 2003. It was adapted for broadcast on BBC Radio 4. **Eden** has been awarded Best New Play and Best Actress (Catherine Walsh) at The Irish Times /ESB Theatre Awards 2001, the Stewart Parker Best New Play Award 2001 and the Rooney Prize for Literature 2003. In 2003 **Eden** was translated into Dutch and Romanian and has been produced in both Amsterdam and Bucharest. The Irish Repertory Theatre New York has just finished a very successful run of the play in March of this year.

Conall Morrison *Director*

Conall's productions for the Abbey Theatre include his own adaptation of Patrick Kavanagh's **Tarry Flynn,** (also at Lyttleton Theatre, Royal National Theatre), Boucicault's **The Colleen Bawn** (also Lyttleton Theatre), **The Freedom of the City, The Tempest, The House, A Whistle in the Dark, Ariel, In a Little World of Our Own, As the Beast Sleeps** and **Twenty Grand**. Other productions include **Conquest of the South Pole, The Marlboro Man, Emma, Measure for Measure, Macbeth** and **Kvetch** and for the Lyric, Belfast, **Dancing at Lughnasa, Juno and the Paycock, Conversations on a Homecoming** and **Ghosts**. He directed **Martin Guerre** for Cameron Mackintosh, touring England and America. His own plays include **Rough Justice, Green, Orange and Pink** and **Hard to Believe**.

Bláithín Sheerin *Designer*

Bláithín's previous work at the Abbey and Peacock Theatres includes **The Drawer Boy, On Such as We, The Sanctuary Lamp, The Morning After Optimism, Baileguangaire, Eden, Made in China, As the Beast Sleeps** and **You Can't Take It With You**. Other designs include **The Comedy of Errors,** RSC, **Our Father,** Almeida Theatre, **The Importance of Being Earnest,** West Yorkshire Playhouse, **The Cavalcaders, Juno and the Paycock,** Lyric Theatre, **The Beckett Festival,** Gate Theatre, John Jay Theatre, New York. Her designs for Rough Magic Theatre Company include **Midden, The Whisperers, The School for Scandal, Northern Star, Pentecost, The Way of the World, The Dogs, Digging for Fire, Love and a Bottle** and **Olga**.

Ian Scott *Lighting Designer*

Ian has designed the lighting for many theatre productions throughout the UK and Europe. Recent theatre includes **Young Europe,** Polka Theatre & Company of Angels, **Slamdunk,** Nitro, **8ooom,** Suspect Culture, **Taylors Dummies,** Gecko and **Peeling,** Graeae.
Other theatre credits include **Henry IV,** Peacock Theatre, **Oh What a Lovely War,** Royal National Theatre, **Skeletons of Fish,** LIFT, **Frogs,** Cottesloe, RNT, **The Lament for Arthur Cleary,** 7:84, **Stalinland,** Citizens Theatre, **Cue Deadly,** Riverside Studios, **The Beauty Queen of Leenane,** Tron Theatre, **Blown,** The Drum, Plymouth and **Crazy Horse,** Paines Plough. Ian is an Associate Artist with Suspect Culture and a regular collaborator with Opera Circus, the David Glass Ensemble and the pioneering theatre company, Graeae.

Steve Blount *Podge*

Steve's theatre credits include numerous performances with such companies as the Abbey and Peacock Theatres, the Northcott Theatre, Exeter, Tinderbox, the Lyric, the Queens Arts Festival and Replay, the Pavilion, the Gaiety, the National Theatre, London, New Balance Dance, Island, The Ark, Blue Raincoat, Meridian, Storytellers, Graffiti, Corn Exchange, the Liverpool Playhouse, Pan Pan, Bickerstaffe, the Theatre Factory, Houston, Texas, La Jolla Playhouse, San Diego, CA and 65 St. Theatre, Seattle, WA. Film and television credits include **Bachelors Walk, Fair City, Glenroe, The Colleen Bawn, Agnes Browne, Mad about Mambo, Pips, Space Truckers, Johnny Loves Suzy** and **Though the Sky Falls**.

Fergal McElherron *David*

Fergal's previous work at the Abbey includes **The House** and **Iphigenia at Aulis**. Other theatre includes **Olga,** Rough Magic, **Mojo Mickybo,** Kabosh (Best Actor, Dublin Fringe Festival 1998 and Best Actor nominee, Irish Times/ESB Theatre Awards 1999), **Candide,** Performance Corporation (Best Actor, Dublin Fringe Festival 2002 and Best Supporting Actor, Irish Times/ESB Theatre Awards 2003), **Trainspotting,** Common Currency, **Starchild and Other Stories,** Storytellers. Film and television credits include Sean Michael in **The Secret of Roan Inish,** Slat Stone in **Eureka Street,** Frank Hughes in **66 Days** and Roy in **Holy Cross**.

Jim Norton *Andy*

Jim's credits at the Abbey and Peacock Theatres include **Red Roses for Me, Tarry Flynn, She Stoops to Folly, Boss Grady's Boys** and **White Woman Street**. He performed in **The Playboy of the Western World, Hamlet, Tamburlaine, St Joan, Comedians, Way Upstream** and **Emigres** at the National Theatre, London and in New York, **The Weir,** Walter Kerr Theater, **Dublin Carol,** Atlantis Theater and **Juno and the Paycock,** Roundabout Theater. Films include **Hidden Agenda, Into the West, Memoirs of an Invisible Man, Conspiracy of Silence, The Oyster Farmer**. For the centenary of Bloomsday Jim has recorded James Joyce's **Ulysses**. Jim is a proud member of Irish Actors Equity since 1957.

John Olohan *Pax*

John trained at the Abbey School of Acting. Work at the Abbey and Peacock Theatres includes **Big Maggie, Moving, Drama at Inish, Sive, Chamber Music, The Field, Dancing at Lughnasa, The House, The Shadow of a Gunman, The Duty Master, Purgatory** and **The Muesli Belt**. At the Gate Theatre, he performed in **Our Country's Good, Romeo and Juliet, The Threepenny Opera, Aristocrats, Sharon's Grave** and **Rough for Theatre 1** and **2**. Other work includes **The Salvage Shop** and **Mackerel Sky**, Red Kettle, **The Buddhist of Castleknock**, Fishamble and **The Chastitute, Moll** and **Canaries** for Edward Farrell Productions. John played Finbar Ryan in **Glenroe**.

Karen Scully *Liz*

Karen completed a degree at Trinity College, Dublin and trained at the Gaiety School of Acting. Previous performances at the Abbey and Peacock Theatres include **Down the Line** and **The Adventures of Shay Mouse**. Other theatre work includes **Buddleia, Native City**, Passion Machine, **St Agunas** – an improvised soap opera, **Borstal Boy**, Gaiety Theatre, **The Plough and the Stars**, Garrick Theatre, West End and UK Tour, **The Witches**, Olympia Theatre, **A Doll's House**, Gate Theatre and a tour of **Gulliver's Travels**, she also sang in the **Burt Backer Act** at Andrews Lane Theatre. She spent the last year touring with **Alone It Stands**. Her television and film work includes **Fair City, The Morbegs, The Family** and **With or Without You**.

abbeyonehundred sponsors

The Abbey Theatre gratefully acknowledges the following for their generous support of **abbey**onehundred.

The Arts Council

Department of Arts, Sport and Tourism

Department of Education and Science

Dermot F Desmond

Moya Doherty

Lew Glucksman and Loretta Brennan Glucksman

The Ireland Funds

John McColgan

Bernard McNamara

The National Lottery

Denis O'Brien

Bord Gáis

Gaiety Theatre

The Heritage Council

Today FM

Tower Records

Savoy

Characters

Andy
David
Pax
Podge
Liz

The play is set in the Savoy Cinema, Edenderry, in 1995.

Act One

A pair of red cinema curtains are closed across the stage. A classic Bernard Herrmanesque film score swells up in the auditorium. This plays until it is reaching its climax, then fades out as the curtains open to reveal a small cinema foyer, with glass doors to stage right and box office to stage left. Stairs jut out to the left of the box office, and disappear round a corner. There is a poster for ACE VENTURA, PET DETECTIVE *on the back wall, near a portrait of an old movie star. A fake chandelier hangs in the middle.* **Andy**, *early sixties, sits on his stool beside the box-office window, looking out through the glass doors to the town square just beyond.* **David**, *late twenties, leans against the stairs, smoking. Car headlights and engine sounds fade up and away through the glass doors.*

David   *Ace Ventura . . .*

Andy   Ah, stop . . .

David   *Ace* fucking *Ventura . . .*

Andy   Lord Jaysus . . .

David   *Pet . . .*

Andy   Fuckin' . . .

David   *Detective . . .*

Andy   Stop.

They pause. David takes a drag on his cigarette.

David   Of all the . . .

Andy   Stop . . .

David   To close with . . .

Andy   Fuckin' . . .

David   *Ace Ventura . . .*

Andy   *Pet Detective . . .* sure don't brown me . . .

David   Sad . . .

Andy   . . . sad night.

David   Sad.

Andy   Sad dose . . .

David   Sad. What would you have liked to have seen?

Andy   Wha'?

David   For the closing film?

Andy   Oh Jeez, anythin', lord lamb a . . . *The Godfathers*, any of them . . . bar the third one, a course!

Andy / David   Shite!

Andy   *Goodfellas, Once Upon a Time in . . .*

Andy   . . . *America* . . .

David   . . . *the West.*

Andy   Either of them. They were both great shows . . . And of course . . . 'You see my mule, he got all riled up when you men fired those shots at his feet . . .'

Andy / David   'You see, I understand that you men were just playin' around, but the mule, he just doesn't get it . . .'

David   Oh Jesus, yeah, I mean yeah . . .

Andy   *A Fistful* . . .

David   Yeah . . . Anything except fucking *Ace Ventura* . . .

Andy   . . . *Pet*, Jaysus, *Detective* . . .

David   Yeah.

David *takes out two plastic cups from a pocket in his coat, a half-bottle of vodka from another pocket, and then a bottle of Coke from an inside pocket.* **Andy** *stares at this.*

Andy   Be Jaysus . . . a cocktail bar in a coat.

David *pours a measure of vodka into one cup, then adds a dash of Coke from the bottle. He offers it across to* **Andy**.

David   For the night that's in it.

Andy   No, I'm . . . No . . . I'll take a drop later on, maybe, when we're . . . when we have to lock up.

David   Come on will ye, have to get the wake started . . .

Andy   I suppose . . . yeah, it is a wake of sorts.

David   Of course it is . . . so . . .

After a beat **Andy** *takes the cup.* **David** *then fixes his own drink.*

It's our duty to get a bit drunk and talk shite about the deceased.

Andy   You're right a mhic.

Andy *gets off his stool and stands in front of the doors, looking out at the town.*

Look at . . .

David   What?

Andy   . . . fuckin' oddball Barney . . . look at him . . . hobblin' across the square . . .

David   Oddball?

Andy   Cunt got ball cancer last year, they had to cut one out . . . Serves him . . . him and his videos, jeez. Used t' cripple us. Under the counter, ye know . . . fuckin' *Rocky Three* . . . 'Ah sure, I seen that on video four months ago.' The business we lost 'cause a that. But ye know, we hung on somehow until . . . aaahhh . . . the lot of them . . . They could have . . . fuckin' . . . supported us more, jeez. They'll all give out now, give out shite that it's gone.

David   Yeah, but . . .

Andy   But fuckin' nothin', fifty-six pound we took in tonight, fifty-six . . . and it the last night . . .

David   Tallaght, forty-five minutes in a car, no waitin' around for new releases . . .

Andy   Ah, only there five year, we're here forty-five year.
Multiplex, multi-fuckin'-my-hole. Where's the . . . personal,
ye know, touch, friendly word . . . 'Oh yeah, hear it's a very
good show all right.' Bit of, 'Jeez, Therese, ye won't see much
of the film if that fella gets ye in the back row' . . . bit of
craic. Up there . . . no way. Remember we met up there
that time, checkin' it out . . . tear of a ticket, a grunt, end of
Johnnymagorry, not worth a hat of . . . And as for the
crowd . . . don't get me . . . The whisperin', talkin' all the
way through . . . as if they were at home watchin' fuckin' . . .
and of course nothin' said, not a word said to shut them up.
Lord lamb of . . . I was boilin'. If I'd had . . . (*Indicates his
torch.*) . . . be the holies, I'd have blinded them and then . . .
(*Swings the torch as if delivering a blow.*) I'd put manners on
them.

David   They have the Dolby Stereo . . .

Andy   Ahhh, don't . . . Who the fuck . . . whose side are
you on? Dolby Stereo, who hit ye? . . . So fuckin' loud ye
can't hardly hear yourself . . . actors roarin' and shoutin'
over explosions, car crashes . . . ear drums turnin' to fuckin'
shite. Dolby . . . imagine havin' to listen to that Jim Carrey
cunt in Dolby-fuckin'-Stereo . . . But if that's what people
want, grand, if that's what ye want . . . that's what ye'll get.

He slams shut one of the glass doors and returns to his stool.

Anyways, it was great ye could make it down, Davy . . .
I was delighted.

David   Wouldn't have missed it . . .

Andy   Be Jaysus a mhic, I'd a . . . honest to God, been
fierce vexed with ye if ye had.

David   Well, there was no way I was going to . . .

Andy   It was just with ye not bein' home this long time . . .

David   . . . going to miss the last . . .

Andy   . . . I was afraid that ye might a been too busy or . . .

David (*rather sharply*) I'm telling you I wouldn't have missed being down here.

He indicates the glass in his hand.

I mean, someone has to make sure that we have a proper wake for the place.

Andy Ah sure, I know, Davy . . .

David I mean, sorry it's been a bit of a while since . . .

Andy Ah, now in fairness, fair play, you bein' the busy, big-time TV star . . .

David It's only a . . . shite people watch with their tea.

Andy Fuck it, gives a lotta people enjoyment . . . Jeez, ol' Mag Moore, up beside us, she lives for it. Poor ol' cunt is that lonely, ye know, lives for it . . . She'd nearly ask me for me autograph 'cause she knows I know ye . . . thinks it's real, that you are a teacher, poor ol' . . . as far as she's concerned that's what you do. Poor ol' . . . gas but . . .

David Gas.

Andy Thinks it's real . . . convinced. Hectic enough now, I'd say.

David It is, yeah.

Andy Yeah, I thought that . . .

David Busy enough . . .

Andy I reckoned that. Of course, people thinks it's easy, people is . . . haven't a clue, ye know, that it's not work, but I know, from you . . . that it is . . . I have the rale angle on it, from the horse's . . . ye know so.

David Can be long enough days, alright.

Andy Have a pain in me bojangles . . . sick tellin' people that . . . I always knew ye'd make it. Even as a young . . . fella, all your voices and everythin' ye used t' do . . .

David Sure, wasn't I the gas little man . . .

Andy   Just want to say that I'm . . . think you're . . . I'm fuckin' proud of ye, is what I'm tryin' to say . . .

David   Well, thanks . . .

Andy   I'm proud of ye this long time.

Andy *raises his glass to* **David** *and with a huge grin drinks to him.* **David** *smiles back, drains his glass and moves away to fix another drink.*

David   So, eh . . . What's . . . what's keepin' Pax tonight?

Andy   Don't know, as ye know yourself he'd usually be Speedy Gonzalez, out the door for the pint.

David   Well, I suppose for once he's takin' his time, his last night beside the projector.

Andy   He seemed to be a bit agitated earlier on. He seemed to be . . . you know the way he does get sometimes. Then when the film was up and runnin' I walked into the projection box and he was . . . be Jaysus . . . on his . . . on the floor, on his hands and knees, sayin' that he'd lost somethin'. What? says I. A watch, says he. So I left him at it, a gnoc that'd lose his head only it's, ye know . . . a course he thinks *Ace Ventura* is the best film of all time, laughs like a child at it. The pint is callin' . . . he won't be too long.

A pause. They watch the town square.

No sign of this young one of yours. Where is she at all?

David   She could be a while yet.

Andy   Jeez, herself and meself got on like a house on . . . that one time she was down . . . fire, be Jaysus . . . Come here, show us the photo again.

David   Every time with this guy, with the photo I have to . . .

David *takes out his wallet, takes out a passport-size photo and hands it to* **Andy**.

Andy A smashin' lookin' bird, even better lookin' in the flesh. The craic we had that time she was down, when I was finally clappin' eyes on her. A picture, be Jaysus, should be in the pictures . . . and the singin's goin' well for her?

Andy *hands back the photo.*

David Very busy, yeah, big gig last night. The launch of her new band . . . and another one tonight.

Andy She'll be down after it, but . . .

David That's what she said, she'll jump in the car . . .

Andy Oh, she'll be down so . . . Would ye ever get her up that fuckin' aisle and don't be actin' the beeswax . . . If I was thirty years younger I'd have her inside in that back row . . . by Jaysus, she's . . . She is . . .

David Careful now, Andy . . .

Andy She is . . .

David . . . the love of my life.

Andy She is . . . Jaysus, when she was here that time, hah . . . hah . . .

David Hah . . . what?

Andy You went inside to watch the film, and she, be Jaysus, stayed out here with me, for a good hour, yarnin' . . . havin' a great time . . .

David She did . . .

Andy Did she, she seemed to . . . ?

David She had a great time . . .

Andy Great . . . only I, ah, was delighted to talk to her . . .

David I was delighted that ye were getting on so well . . .

Andy So ye weren't browned like that she stayed out with me . . . ?

David Why the fuck would I . . . ?

Andy   I just kinda felt a funny . . . that you were a bit, don't know, off with me, when the two of you were leavin'.

David   Really? Sorry if . . .

Andy   Ah, no . . .

David   If you thought that . . . must have been tired or something . . .

Andy   Yeah . . . yeah . . . the long hours. Any word from the da?

David   My da . . . oh yeah, he . . . he was asking for you, Andy.

Andy   (*slight pause*) Was he . . .?

David   Yeah . . . he was on tonight from London. Wished you well. I think he was getting a bit choked up over the phone . . . thinking of his father, the two of them driving home to Williamstown together, and his father turning to him and saying, 'We're buyin' the cinema, son.' . . . I think he feels very bad now having to sell. Had to be done . . .

Andy   Sacrilege, but . . . absolute sacrilege . . . to think of a builders' providers inside there.

David   Nothing he could . . . just couldn't afford to keep it going . . . I suppose the whole town has it that he's . . . in difficulties?

Andy   Ah . . . I do get grilled the odd time, alright . . . It's a fuckin' . . . a shame that he couldn't . . . have at least made it over, for the last night.

David   Well, he said that he'd been thinkin' about here all day . . . the old days. You and Jackie Shiel . . . the Saturday morning *Flash Gordons* . . .

Andy   Jaysus, the *Flash Gordons* . . . kids packed into the front, the pit, ye know, and the bold Jackie demonstratin' to me how to keep control, any messin' met by the back of Jackie's hand.

David   And the dancin', Andy . . . No wake would be complete without the . . .

In a flash **Andy** *is off his stool.*

Andy   The fuckin' dancin'! Jackie standin' out here, right here beside the box office, greetin' the top of the queue, queues in those days be Jaysus . . . a word for everyone, personal touch, ye know. Then he'd choose a . . . a young one . . . he'd bow the head, ask her to . . . 'Would ye care for the next dance, madam?' Boyfriend, husband, lookin' on like gomies as Jackie did a short little waltz round the foyer with their loved one. A great mover he was, for a big man. So there was this kinda suspense when you were queuein' up, who would Jackie pick out? No one let on, but everyone was thinkin' about it . . . I mean, I used t' be there in the queue with Marie, I'd be there thinkin' of Jackie, silver-tongued Jackie, Gary-fuckin'-Cooper-Jackie, man of the world . . . I'd be there, thinkin' what if he never picks my woman out, what did that say . . . about . . . her . . . 'cause he hadn't yet asked her. Jeez, the Sunday nights I spent prayin' that he would . . . 'cause I knew that Marie was conscious of it, I knew that. Well, so's anyways, thank the lord lamb a . . . on Marie's nineteenth birthday, a big night out, *The Robe* was on, huge crowd, all the way round the Town Hall, and Jackie made his move. Marie's face lit up like a . . . Took his hand, movin' around the foyer with Jackie . . . like a . . . lit up like a Christmas tree. Someone in the queue shouted 'Happy birthday,' another friend started up a 'Happy birthday to you' . . . I was kinda annoyed that I hadn't started up the song, hadn't thought of it . . . vexed, so I didn't join in until the last 'Dear Marie, happy birthday to you'. Everyone clappin', Marie beamin', face red as a . . . Jackie, big broad grin, takin' a bow. Later that night Richard Burton was converted to Christianity and we all filed out the doors as happy as pigs in shite.

David   Out into the night. Walked her home then, didn't ye . . . to her door?

Andy I did . . . to her door at a certain time, 'cause her da was fierce strict. She wasn't allowed do nothin' . . .

David But you took her away from all that . . .

The sound of doors opening and closing from the top of the stairs.

Andy I did.

Andy *looks up towards the noise. We hear huffing and puffing and feet descending the stairs with great effort. Andy returns to his stool.*

Ho oh, here we are now . . .

The two men wink to each other as **Pax**, *late fifties, appears round the last bit of stairs lugging two large tin boxes with 'Ace Ventura' handwritten in marker-pen on the sides.*

Pax Deadly boys, fuckin' deadly, said the rat when he ate the poison . . . that Jim Carrey is . . . Lord jeez, strangled I am . . .

David Here, Pax, let me . . .

Andy Leave him . . .

David *moves up onto the steps and takes one one of the boxes from* **Pax**.

Pax Thanks, David . . .

They continue down the last few steps and deposit the boxes at the bottom.

Pax There now . . . last time I'll ever have to . . . I tell ye though, boys, that Jim Carrey is some man for one man, the faces he does do, mouth like fuckin' elastic . . . this class of a fuckin' monkey boys, leps onto him, bites into his bollocks, the roars of him, well, I'm not coddin' or jokin' ye's now, but . . . great show, boys, a rale good ol' laugh. Well, that's her . . . the last of them. Sad like, but . . . I won't miss that fuckin' stairs. Anyways I'm slippin' on across . . .

Andy For the pint.

Pax The pint, ye'd need a pint on a night like tonight.

David Ye would.

Pax Sad dose, anyways there's an ol' soccer meetin' on over there . . .

David It can wait, Pax.

Pax Ah now, I'm the treasurer, ye know . . .

David Come on, Pax, a final toast to the place.

David *lifts up the vodka and produces another plastic cup.*

Pax Jeez, ye have . . .

David On tap.

Pax Ah no, I'd better . . .

David Pax . . .

Pax . . . not, 'cause Willy Muirin has some big announce-ment to make . . .

David I'm insisting.

He pours a measure into the cup.

Pax With any luck the bollocks is resignin' . . .

David How long have . . .?

Pax . . . so I really should be . . .

David How long have you been showin' pictures here?

Pax . . . there to hear. Wha?

Andy Ah, he's only here a wet week.

Pax Sha' up, you . . . Oh, oh jeez . . . I must be here, well, fifteen . . .

Andy Fourteen year.

Pax Fourteen year?

David Fourteen, fifteen, whatever . . . the fucking soccer club can wait ten minutes.

*He hands **Pax** the cup.*

Pax   Sure, I suppose, as the fella says . . . it is a sad night.

Andy   'Tis.

Pax   'Tis.

David   It is.

David *pours some Coke into Pax's mug.*

Pax   Wha' is it?

David   Smirnoff, drop of Coke.

Pax   Be the jiminees, don't usually now, but . . .

David   Right, men, I propose a toast.

Andy   Right, right, raise yer . . . yer . . . plastic cups.

David   To the Savoy . . . and all who sailed in her.

Andy / Pax   The Savoy.

They all take a drink.

David   May she rest in peace.

Pax   How's the da? Haven't seen much of him round the town.

David   Up to his eyes, in London, a lot going on, so he has to . . . be over there.

Pax   And how's everythin' goin' for him?

David   Ah, you know yourself . . . grand.

Andy   Ye were up there a while, Pax. Normally ye'd, be Jaysus, bolt, ye know, straight away, like a rat out of a . . . bolt for to get to the pint . . .

Pax   Just, ye know . . . tidyin' stuff away . . .

Andy   Is that right? A bit late to be gettin' . . . and the place closin' . . . neat and tidy now, and it the last . . .

Pax   I always kept a clean projection box . . .

David   Andy, hey, Andy, bit of sensitivity for this man, on the night that's in it. How many reels of film have you dealt with, have you shown to this town over the years?

Pax   Ah, Lord, I wouldn't know.

David   Hundreds.

Pax   I suppose.

David   So you couldn't blame a man for takin' his time putting away his last reel of film, now could ye?

Andy   I think he was at somethin' else up there . . .

Pax   Jeez . . . you know everything . . .

Andy   Tick-tock, tick-tock . . .

Pax   Jaysus . . .

Andy   Tick-tock . . . Still pokin' around up there after the . . .

Pax   Yeah . . . okay. I am, as it happens . . .

David   After . . .

Andy   Tick-tock . . .

Pax   I'm after mis-fuckin'-placin' this watch, David. It's just that Rita'll go on the warpath. Her skin and blister got us a pair of matchin' lady's and gent's watches for the anniversary five year ago. She'll skin me if it doesn't turn up and that is the truth.

David   We'll keep an eye out.

Andy   Skin ye, she will.

David   We won't leave here tonight without it.

Andy *gets up off his stool and heads for the doors. He stops and turns to address* **David**.

Andy   Jaysus, I nearly forgot, your old enemy Jimbob Hickey was in the other night . . . with the fiancée Fiona Dunne . . . and we had great craic, I was sittin', ye know, havin' the chat while they were gettin' the tickets, and who comes in behind them only the Hopper Hynes, and he used go with Fiona for years, so I'm slaggin' him that the better man won and all this, and had the Hopper no woman now, 'cause he'd only walked in with his brother, the Hippo Hynes, and we all . . . a great laugh . . . had a great bit of craic . . . the ol' personal, ye know, touch . . . can't beat it . . . people does love that . . . and Jimbob Hickey, new leaf, no more fightin' or messin', all done up and holdin' hands. Of course this man here was the one of the few to ever win a row with him . . . (*Indicates* **David.**)

David   Andy, I wouldn't . . .

Andy   Ye did . . .

Pax   Ye did not, ye bet Jimbob . . . go 'way from me . . .

Andy   I'm tellin' ye that he fuckin' did . . .

David   We were only kids, Pax . . .

Andy   He was tryin' to bully him, but you was havin' none of it . . . that right, Davy?

David   That's right.

Pax *drains his cup and goes for the doors.*

Pax   Jaysus . . . Right, I'll vamoose on over . . .

David   Listen, Andy, I wouldn't mind nipping over to Mac's with Pax for a proper pint . . . just a quick one.

Andy   Ye will in your . . . shite . . . No way Jose. Ye'll stay here, at the wake . . . Christ, Davy, ye can go to the pub any night . . . but not tonight, surely not? Let him go across, but you stay here . . .

David   Okay . . . grand, just fancied a pint . . . I won't move.

Andy   Anyways, I . . . I have to . . . slip across to the phone box and give Marie a ring to remind her that I'll be hangin' on for a bit . . . the night that's in it. I already told her, but ye know the way she does be . . . the way she does . . .

David (*indicating box office*)   Can ye not from the . . .

Pax   Ah, the phone here was cut off months ago.

David   Oh, right . . . we'll hold the fort so.

Pax   Who's we? I have to . . .

David   Last night, Pax. Come on . . . the wake.

Pax   Jaysus . . . Ye'd swear someone had died.

Andy   Back in a sec.

Andy *leaves through one of the doors.* **David** *and* **Pax** *look out after him.*

Pax   Lord Jaysus, he's like a class of an over-excited child at his own birthday party or somethin'.

David   What'll he do with himself . . .?

Pax   True, kept him occupied for years, sure, what else did he ever have?

Pax *leans up against the box office beside Andy's stool They continue to gaze out of the doors at the square.*

So how's the telly gettin' on?

David   Good . . . yeah.

Pax   Gone to twice a week now, isn't it?

David   The two, yeah.

Pax   I do see it the odd time, but Rita . . . Rita'd never miss it . . .

They watch as car lights fade up and away outside.

Twice a week . . .

David   Yeah, tougher schedule now.

Pax   Ye mean ye's have longer hours sittin' in that pub drinkin' pints and gettin' paid for it . . .

David   Fuck off!

Pax   It is rale beer, isn't it? They do all ask me that beyond in Mac's . . .

David   It is.

Pax   I told them that . . . paid to drink beer. Jaysus . . .

David   It's poxy shite, lyin' there all week . . . Just try . . . try takin' a slug of it at eight o'clock in the morning with a hangover.

Pax   Well, God love ye's . . . Seriously though, I wouldn't mind takin' a slug outta that new young one . . . wha' . . . wha' . . . I'd give her some scourgin'. Great little body on her . . . wha'?

David   Better in real life . . . up close.

Pax   Ye bollocks, ye . . . and your . . . your . . . whadye-callit . . . character is gettin' fierce pally with her, are ye goin' to get to shift her?

David   Don't know, haven't seen the next batch of scripts yet, so . . .

Pax   Ye lucky . . . jammy. Oh, be Jaysus, looky over there, see, passin' by Paddy's pit-stop, see . . . the ram Ryan. Wait till I . . . One of the boys in the tyre factory was tellin' me Ram was . . .

Pax *takes a swallow of his drink and slips up onto Andy's stool.*

Ram was up in Dublin, not this long ago, at a nightclub, and he meets a quare one and brings her outside into the back of his van, him fairly gee-eyed . . . so he's goin' at her, good-oh, like . . . for ages and not a thing happenin' for him, like all Ram wants to do is shoot his load, ye know, and get home, like he's work in the morning . . . so she goes down and starts givin' him an ol' . . . Billy Joel, ye know, and she's doin' her level best . . . but still no sign of ne'er a tadpole and the Ram is gettin' browned, so he says to your one, 'That's great what you're doin' but let a man's hand at that.' He pushes her head out of the way and gives himself a . . . a hand-shandy in front of her . . .

David Fuck . . .

Pax 'Let a man's . . . hand at that . . .'

David And did he manage to . . . in the end . . .?

Pax I don't . . . I presume he did . . .

They are now both in fits of laughter, bursting, as **Andy** *re-enters by the front doors. He glares across at* **Pax** *who promptly slides off* **Andy***'s stool, the laughter still going.* **Andy** *walks across and takes up his rightful place, but does not for a second acknowledge the high amusement of the other two.*

David Everything all right?

Andy Yeah. Said I'd be home before twelve.

David She alright?

Andy Yeah . . .

Pax *makes a move towards the doors.*

Pax Right, thanks for the sup, I'll see ye's later.

Andy Ye'll be back over for the watch, or Rita will have your guts for garters . . .

Pax *ignores this and opens one of the doors to go out.*

Andy Jaysus, Davy, did I ever tell ye about the time Jackie barred Rita and Pax from here?

Pax *pauses at the open door.*

Andy He told me that they were gettin' up to all sorts in the back row, settin' a bad example . . . He had to bar them for six months . . . until they cooled off, ha . . .

Pax doesn't move for a beat, then shuts the door and turns back round to Andy.

Pax Is that what he said . . .?

Andy   He did.

Pax   Did he? Well now, I'll tell ye a thing . . . One night me and Rita were here after seein' a film, the crowd filin' out, and I go into the jacks and Rita is standin' here, just there where you are, Davy, and the bold Jackie comes up behind her and makes a . . . suggestion to her . . . and Rita told him to fuck right off and so Jackie got thick and he . . .

Andy   No way . . . would ye go 'way? I won't have Jackie's name, on the night that's in it . . . his name taken in vain.

Pax   Arrah . . . look, that's what he was like, sure everyone knew it.

Andy   By Jaysus, Davy, he was a great man . . . Lord have mercy on him, should be remembered tonight. Christ, the place was never the same after he . . . then this fella took over.

David, *anxious to keep the peace, fills* **Pax***'s cup and then* **Andy***'s.*

David   When would that have been, Pax, when you started here?

Pax   Ah, '81, '82 . . . just after the revamp. The new seats and that.

Andy   Lord have . . . *Chariots of Fire* . . . last film that Jackie ever reeled up . . .

Pax   I saw that months before it came here, oddball Barney had a pirate . . .

Andy   Fuckin' pirates . . .

David (*to Pax*)   Can you remember the first film you ever reeled up?

Andy   There's no way Jose that he'd remember that.

Pax   Shut up, you.

Andy   Fiver says ye can't.

Pax   Will ye shut up while I think.

Andy   Couldn't, be Jaysus, his own name.

Pax   I think it was a cops-and-robbers . . .

David   Early eighties . . . English or American?

Pax   I . . . bastard of a . . . to be honest, I . . .

David   *Long Good Friday* . . .

Pax   I'm not bein' . . . now, but . . . I haven't the faintest.
Cops-and-robbers, I think it was.

David   Jesus, you're useless, Pax.

Andy   Knew it . . . fiver.

Pax   Would you ever?

Andy   A fiver.

Pax   Would you ever . . . did ye see me spittin' on me
hand and shakin' . . .?

Andy   No .

Pax   No, ye didn't, so no . . . no fiver.

Andy   It was, for your information, *Venom.*

Pax / David   *Venom?*

Andy   *Venom* . . . Oliver Reed has this family kidnapped in a
house, cops outside, but there's a class of a deadly poisonous
snake on the loose inside in the house . . .

Pax   Must be some space inside in the head to fit shite the
like of that in it . . .

Andy   Just 'cause ye couldn't . . .

Pax   Well, there was cops in it, wasn't there . . .

David   Close enough, Pax.

Andy   Ahhhh.

Andy *turns away in disgust and lights a smoke.*

David   Well, I'll tell ye, boys, it's as clear to me, the first
time that I ever set foot in here . . . 1973, seven years of age,
The Sound of Music at the Saturday matinee, and then Dad

the next Friday night brought me over to show me inside the projection box, which was a big deal, 'cause I'd been let up late, big deal at that age. And Jackie Shiel was there and so was Dustin Hoffman, kissin' a woman's tits . . . Jackie sayin' that a young fella like me shouldn't be witnessin' the likes of that, Dad winding up Jackie, saying something like, sure a man and a woman together, isn't it only a natural thing . . . My dad laughing, he used t' have a great laugh . . . in . . . those days . . . Jackie not impressed . . .

Andy   Well, he wouldn't have been . . . X-rated it was, and you only a gasoon . . .

Pax   Like you or Jackie gave a bollocks when it came to the matinees.

Andy   Well, sure, what could ye do, in those days? If there was no Disney or anythin' suitable sent down, ye had to peg on whatever was there.

David   Fucking brilliant it was, some of the stuff we ended up seeing . . . Four hundred kids off our heads on Coke, crisps and Captain Hurricane bars, stampin' our feet if the reel broke . . .

Andy   I fuckin' remember ye . . . Jackie splicin' it back together as quick as he could . . .

David   Whistling whenever James Bond went in for the snog . . .

Andy   And Jaysus, afterwards, the sight of ye all burstin' out onto the square . . .

David   Chargin' towards the Town Hall . . .

Andy   Stone mad, be Jaysus.

David   High-kickin' the shite out of each other.

Andy   Ye'd seen a Bruce Lee . . .

David   Walkin' as if we'd shit in our pants.

Andy   Shit in your . . .?

David *demonstrates walk.*

David Fill your hands, you son of a bitch.

Andy A John Wayne . . .

David Squintin' our eyes and . . .

Andy A Clint . . .

David Fightin' invisible skeletons!

Andy The whadyemacallit?

David *Jason and the* . . .

Andy The . . . the . . . the . . . fuckin' *Argonauts.*

David Running and falling in slow motion . . . mimin' blood explodin' out of our chests . . .

Andy *The Wild Bunch*!

David IF THEY MOVE . . .

Andy / David . . . KILL 'EM!

David The most violent western of all time.

Pax *has been half-listening, but mostly studying the town square.*

Pax All I know is that ye's used t' leave the most violent fuckin' mess behind ye's. Ye'd have poor ol' Siddy Nolan strangled cleanin' up after ye, he used t' be always givin' out about ye . . . 'Bloody little buggers, jeppers a man, they have chewin' gum walked into the carpets, seats destroyed from mineridils . . .' Davy, Christ, I remember when we took his bike . . . after Offaly won the All-Ireland in '82, Mucky Meehan and a few of us, and we painted it green, white and yella, and him pure Royal County, pure Meath.

Andy That was a bastard of a thing to . . .

Pax It was only takin' a hand, and sure he had ten years of gloatin' after it, the faithful winnin' fuck-all and Meath, All-Irelands to bate the band . . .

Andy Up above in Offalia House now, poor ol' dickens.
Wouldn't know ye now, wouldn't know anyone. But sure . . .
Poor ol' whoor . . . Davy, he used t' come here after every
show for to clean . . .

David Yeah, sure I remember him . . .

Andy But like, on his one night off he still came down
here, anythin' to get away from Bridgie, the wife, He'd be
here with the St John's Road boys every Monday to watch a
western, all the boys, never missed a Monday, any weather.
Cans a Club Shandy, Mars Bars from Mrs Muarry, and that
was it . . . But one Monday there was nearly a . . . one
Monday . . . Christ, didn't Film House send us down *Diva*,
ye know, the French yoke, good show but . . . not for the
Monday-night western brigade, not for the original fuckin'
Wild Bunch, no way Jose. The rat Finegan comes barrellin'
out after five minutes. 'Lord Jaysus, Andy, what's all that
fuckin' writin' doin' up on the screen?' Be jeanny, there was
murder she wrote . . . The only one of them that stayed was
poor Siddy, not able to read a word, just delighted to be out
from under Bridgie's feet for the night . . . The rest of them
vamoosed, wanted their dollars back too.

David And did they get them?

Andy Who hit ye? Indeedin' they did not.

Pax Sure, this fella wouldn't refund the Pope.

Andy No, nor Father, little bollocky . . . nor to Father
Olly Mac either . . .

Pax Oh, here we go . . .

Andy Years ago . . . the little . . . What was it at all he
was at? Little short-arse, got offended at somethin', wanted
his, ye know . . . back. I says, I says to him, 'Well now,
Father,' I says, 'When I go up to one of your Masses and
leave me few pounds into the collection box, and then I
decide that I don't like your fuckin' sermon, I don't barrel
up the aisle askin' for me few pounds back,' says I to him . . .

Pax   Unbelievable . . .

Andy   I fuckin' did, he was still lookin' at me. 'Good night, now, Father,' says I, and he fucked off, out the door, and waddled on across the square, the little . . .

Pax *shakes his head.* **David** *laughs,* **Andy** *lights a fag.*

Andy   That's what I said to him . . . now.

David *gives him a thumbs up and a wink.*

Pax   Christ.

Andy   That's what I said . . . He didn't set foot in the place for five years.

Pax   Could ye blame the chap?

Andy   Wouldn't have come back at all except he wasn't goin' to miss *Ghandi.*

David   Did *Ghandi* inspire him, Andy, did he take to wearin' a loincloth, start to refuse food until you gave him his refund?

Andy   That little roly-poly would never refuse food.

Pax   Jeez, boys ye's are fuckin' Cat . . .

Andy   Ah would ye . . .

Pax   Cat Malogin, after the man did so much.

Andy   For who?

Pax   For the town.

Andy   Ah what, organised a few ol' youth discos, a half-arsed rag week and a stupid parade every Easter . . .

Pax   Brought people into the town when there was nothin'.

Andy   Listen, if ye saw one fuckin' Abel Alarm float . . .

Pax   Always tryin' to do . . .

Andy   . . . . ye kinda saw them all.

Pax   . . . somethin' for the place.

Andy   He'd never be out of the pubs and halls . . . the golf club . . .

Pax   More than you've ever done . . .

Andy   Who hit ye?

David   To be fair, Andy, there wasn't too many others that ever bothered their holes.

Andy   Him and his committees and meetings . . . this, that and the other . . .

Pax   Well, Christ, if it was left up to the like of you there'd be fuck-all done for fuckin' no one.

Andy   Is that right? That's right, great man was Father Mac, havin' a feel of Carmel Kelly's knee whenever he could, or any other married woman that was in range . . .

Pax   He's a man, isn't he?

Andy   He's not a man, he's a priest. Well, he is a man . . . a man of the cloth, not a man about town the way he did be . . . and I'm one of his flock . . . and I asked him for help . . . I expected that, but no . . . useless . . . great man to arrange all the . . . granted, but what about when ye asked him for real help, the time when Marie, when she was gettin' the way . . . I was at me . . .

Pax   He wasn't a . . . whadyecallit, social worker . . .

Andy   I know that now . . . pure useless. And Maire all pleased, brightened up, 'cause the priest was comin' to visit. Got the tin of USA biscuits down, tea ready, a kind of normality to the house, our . . . home, that the priest does walk into . . . but I knew by the head of him, as soon as he parked his arse that he'd rather have been . . . So he trots out a few load-of-me-hole words of . . . ye know, fuck-all use to her, 'cause she senses that he was . . . that he'd rather be anywhere else. So he leaves, and we're sittin' there, no chat now, she was feelin' worse now, 'cause she felt that she'd embarrassed the priest some way . . . it was worse she improved after that . . .

Pax   Ah, look, it sure I'm sure he did his best . . . can't be easy for them, Andy, put yourself in his shoes.

Andy   Aaarah . . .

Andy   *lights up a smoke and moves away to the doors.*

Pax   How is she this weather?

Andy   Grand, she's grand.

David   Does she still do the garden?

Andy   Yeah, she does, yeah . . .

David   She loved it . . . as a young fella, every week, up in ye're place, I was always brought out and given a running commentary on the latest developments.

Andy   That's right.

David   Although, Pax, he never really approved, he allowed her about half an hour with me, no more . . . thought it was a bit sissish . . .

Andy   I did not . . .

Pax   The big man . . .

Andy   Would ye's feic off . . . anyways, Davy, yeah, she's still mad into it . . . as a matter of fact, only recently, there we were out like . . . pleased as . . . her sweet william . . . as punch . . . made a special effort for to admire what she'd done, a sunflower and all, be Jaysus. In great form, she was . . .

Pax   Good to hear . . . It's just . . . were ye tellin' David about the other week . . .?

Andy   No, I didn't . . .

David   What's this?

Andy   Ah, nothin' . . .

Pax   No it was just my Rita was passin' by their house of
an evenin' and she saw Marie outside, in a bit of a state . . .
She was in the yard to feed ol' Jake and was after lockin'
herself out. So Rita stayed with her until he got back from
here. I'm only askin' 'cause Rita said that she'd been in a
fierce state . . . upset like, very upset . . . Rita said.

Andy   Well, she's grand now, just got a bit of a shock when
she couldn't . . . the door shuttin' on her.

Pax   She cut herself, didn't she, on the tin . . . for the dog?

Andy   She did.

Pax   Her thumb, Rita said.

Andy   She did, yeah . . .

David   Was she alright?

Andy   She's grand . . .

Pax   She's okay?

Andy   It was only her Jaysus thumb, not her throat . . .

David   Good . . . That's good.

Pax   Still doesn't manage the shops . . . no.

Andy   Not at all . . . that was the first to go . . . then the
evenin's out at the bridge. Sure, Christ, as I've said . . . the
way a thing can happen so gradually ye don't realise it . . .
next thing it suddenly dawns on ye that she hasn't been
outside the front door in weeks . . . I mean, the bridge, sure
she loved the bridge.

David   And on Sundays?

Andy   The odd time, about once a month, but I do have
to cajole her. It does do her good, though, when she does . . .
but it's into the chapel and out again and straight home . . .

David   No hangin' round . . .

Andy   For the chat, no . . . and she used t' love that as
well. Ah sure, some days . . . she'd be . . . then other days

she'd be . . . as the fella says . . . anyways, I'd better keep
an eye on the . . . and not get to mickey monk . . . get
home to . . . fix the cocoa and tuck her in . . . keep an eye
on the . . . 'cause we've them posters to sort, too, me letters
to do and inside to be checked.

David We've time enough, don't be fretting.

Andy I think the . . . the night is, be Jaysus . . . is gettin'
to me . . . (*He drains his cup.*) Peg another one in there like a
good child.

David *hands him his drink.* **Andy** *moves back to his stool.*

Pax Kinda thing that it get to ye, alright . . . (**Pax** *keeps his
eyes fixed on* **Andy**.) Don't know how ye do it.

David He's a good man. That right, Andy . . . you'll
always look after her?

Andy Yeah . . . least I can do . . .

Pax For better or for worse . . .

Andy *suddenly breaks from his stool and takes out a cigarette, placing
it in* **David**'s *mouth.*

Andy Come on, Davy . . . 'You see, my mule, he got all
riled up when you men fired those shots at his feet . . .'

David *grins, slips off his coat, turns it around and ties its arms
around his neck, wearing it like a poncho. He slowly takes out matches
and lights the fag in his mouth, squints his eyes and does a very good
Clint impression.*

David 'You see, I understand that you men were just
playin' around, but the mule, he just doesn't get it. Of course
if you were all to apologise . . . I don't think it's nice you
laughin', you see my mule don't like you laughin' . . .'

Andy / David 'Gets the crazy idea that you're laughin' at
him . . . now if you all apologise, like I know you're going
to . . . I might be able to convince him that you really
didn't mean it.'

David *pauses, then flicks his arm out from under the coat and shoots four times.*

Andy   Ha . . . mowed them down, quick as lightnin'.

David   'My mistake . . . four coffins.'

Andy *(clapping his hands)*   Deadly . . . 'My mistake . . . four coffins.' Our favourite, Davy.

David *puts on his coat and takes a drink.*

David   *A Fistful of Dollars* . . .

Andy   *A Fistful of* fuckin' *Dollars* . . .

Pax *drains his cup.*

Pax   Lord Jaysus . . . Port Laoise mental hospital . . .

Andy   You at the bottom of the stair there, Davy, what age would ye have been?

David   Oh, eight or nine, I suppose . . . Creeled myself tryin' to re-enact the ending of it.

Andy   Ballin' like a baba . . .

David   No Mexican baddie ever balled like a baba.

Andy   Well, Pancho Villa, you fuckin' did . . .

David   I know . . .

They smile at each other and hold each other's gaze for a moment. **Pax** *breaks the moment by moving to the doors.*

Pax   I better bowlt across . . .

Andy   Ye'd better . . .

Pax   It'll be comin' to Willy Muirin's speech, hope he resigns . . . such a browner.

Andy   And if he does, Pax, ye reckon you're in with a shout?

Pax   As good a chance as any of them.

Andy   Ye reckon?

Pax   I do . . .

Andy   Dream fuckin' on . . . You'll go over to that soccer meetin' fully expectin', full sure, that your man Willy . . . Willy Muirin will announce his . . . that he's, ye know, steppin' down, and that they'll all, that you'll be elected president . . . and they'll no more . . .

David   He has been there for years.

Andy   Would you put this fella in a position of president, my hole . . .

David   They might . . .

Andy   Ah, would ye . . . who hit ye? You'll go over there now, sip on your ol' pint, full of 'Definitely this year,' and what will happen . . . the Badger or the Mouse will get it ahead of ye . . .

Pax   Maybe they will, but at least I'm goin' to have a go. More than . . . ah, look it . . . wastin' me breath. I'll see ye, David . . .

Andy   You'll be back across later for the watch.

Pax   I'll see, I don't know

Andy   'Cause, Jesus, if it doesn't turn up, and Rita gets hold of ye . . .

Pax   Will you still be here?

Andy   I will . . .

Pax   Well then, I mightn't bother.

Andy   Rita . . .

David   Good luck, Pax . . .

Andy   Rita . . .

Pax *makes his exit. The other two look on after him.*

David   Bit harsh.

Andy   Not at all . . . just tryin' to bring . . . a bit of reality.
He'll be back over . . . don't worry, I know well he will,
afraid of his life of her . . . always was, even when they were
courtin', when we all used t' go to the dances in Dublin, it'd
be, Pax, do this, and Pax, do that . . . I used t' have to
laugh at him . . .

David   Not like you, Andy. You never ran after Marie like
that . . . you wore the trousers, that's right . . .

Andy   That's . . . right.

David   Ye know the thing Pax said about Jackie . . . that
Jackie said something dirty to Rita?

Andy   Never mind that . . .

David   Pax said that everyone knew Jackie was like that . . .

Andy   You don't believe him, do ye?

David   Why would he say it, then?

Andy   He'd make up fuckin' anythin' to save face . . .
Pax's the dirty little article, always was. Jackie enjoyed a
laugh and a joke with the girls, that was all.

*Something has caught **Andy**'s eye in the square.*

Jeez, look over, do ye see who it is . . .

David   Is that Paddy Delaney?

Andy   Comin' out of his pit-stop . . .

David   Who's the woman?

Andy   Well, this is it, not from the town. A Mrs Robinson
from Castlejordan . . .

David (*sings*)   'Here's to you, Mrs Robinson.'

Andy   Husband died last year . . . sure, she has ten years
on Paddy . . . gas but, never hardly been with a woman his
whole life . . . ye'd always see him comin' outta Mac's on
his own . . . Must be . . . hard for people the like a that, in
the pubs or discos . . . But anyways, he met your one, fifty

if she's a day, last year when they were doin' a show with the Boyne Players . . . and now, every Saturday, parks the car, into his shop the two of them, and then an hour later, he drives her home . . . gas but . . .

David They have sex?

Andy Wha' . . .?

David They have sex on the shop counter every Saturday?

Andy I . . . I suppose they do be at somethin' . . . Oh, Jaysus, it's not somethin' that ye'd be . . . not even Pax would get a thrill outta thinkin' about them at it. Oh, stop . . . but do ye know somethin', in all the years I been here and Paddy Delaney only across the square he's never once darkened the Savoy doors. Probably doesn't even know we're closin' . . . Ah sure, better get on with it. You could get the ladder for me . . .

Andy *walks towards and then exits through the auditorium door.* **David** *follows him.* **Andy** *reappears seconds later inside the box office and starts to clear it out, taking down calendars, throwing away old tickets, etc.* **David** *re-emerges into the foyer carrying a stepladder. He sets it down.*

Andy Where the fuck is your young lady . . .?

David God knows . . .

David *drains his cup and goes for another.*

Andy Jaysus, you're fairly mowin' into the . . .

David Fuck it, what else do ye do at a wake?

Andy True enough . . . Anyhow, Emma'll be here soon, with any luck.

Car headlights fade up and sweep across the doors before dying out at the same time as the car engine.

Speakin' of which, who's this now?

David *looks up suddenly, which causes him to spill a little vodka as he pours it into his cup.*

Andy   No, no, I know that Renault . . . that's Podge
Pender and the missus. See them there . . . just parked . . .
they're goin' across to Mac's . . . ye couldn't miss them . . .
Gas but . . . he's be Jaysus six-foot four, a Harlem-fuckin'-
Globetrotter, she's a five-feet-nothin' . . . a . . . an Oompla
Loompla. Been' goin' out since they were in school, our two
most loyal customers. Jeez, every Sunday they've parked the
car in the same spot, this side of the Town Hall. I have the
tickets ready for them as they walk over, I always have to
smile to meself, Little and Large . . . They always have the
exact money, and they always buy the two cans of Coke,
Maltesers and two packets of dry-roasted peanuts, then up
the stairs . . .

Andy *continues his clear-out of the box office, throwing things into a
black plastic bag.*

David   On into the back row . . .

Andy   Where half the fuckin' town was conceived . . . No,
none of that for the Penders any more. Oh Christ, they'd
be strictly marriage-bed material now. No spectator sport
there . . . no late shows for them any more.

David   The late show . . .

Andy   I often thought of not botherin' to show the film at
all, no one would have noticed . . . bet into each other.

David   The late show . . .

Andy   A spectator sport . . . Pax there takin' a good gawp
in at them all. Christ, the time Derek Mahon had his head
between Eilish Moore's legs . . . I shined the torch in at them,
she gives his head a slap and up he pops like a fuckin' . . .
a rabbit caught in the . . .

Andy *re-enters the foyer, takes up the ladder and, during the next
exchange, opens one of the front doors and sets up the ladder outside.
He climbs onto the ladder and begins to hand down plastic letters from
the sign outside to* **David***.*

David   Eilish Moore . . .

Andy   A fine-lookin' bird.

David   Well, I'll tell ye something, Andy.

Andy   Go on.

David   Eilish Moore . . .

Andy   Yeah?

David   . . . was . . .

Andy   Go on.

David   . . . the first girl that I ever . . .

Andy   Yeah?

David   . . . kissed. So there ye are.

Andy   Did ye, ye never brought her . . .?

David   I was supposed to, one Saturday, but I . . .

Andy   I never saw ye here . . .

David   I . . . chickened out.

Andy   Afraid of your shite at what . . .?

David   Lost the nerve . . .

Andy   At the slaggin' that I woulda dished out?

David   No, it wasn't that, it was . . . the other lads were so impressed. They'd all seen me out on the floor with her at the youth club disco, so all the next week in school I was the man, I mean that was the most enjoyable thing about it, not actually snogging her, it was the kudos I was gettin' . . . Eilish had tits like . . . So I did arrange to meet her outside here, but I was scared stiff that I'd fuck it up. I was loving my new-found status with the boys. but the thought of actually having to meet . . . talk to her . . . know when to make the move, all of that . . . The youth club had been fine, it was in the moment, a surprise thing, being pushed together by her friends, ye know, you have the cue, there's no time to think. But the pictures . . . you're taking the penalty, expected to score . . . So there I am, across the square at home, peeping out from behind the curtains, and at five to eight I spot her, standing outside here. I put on me coat, trying not to think, I get outside the back door, cajoling myself to go on, to just walk across the square but I . . . couldn't. Five minutes later I'm back inside peeping through the curtains again, I could still see her, waitin' . . . but I just couldn't . . . For the next twenty minutes or so I kept checking out the window and each time she was still standing there . . . until eventually I saw her walk away, on down the town. I went in and watched *The Late Late Show* with the da, feeling like an absolute cunt . . . Eilish never spoke to me again.

Andy *has taken down all the letters and is standing beside the ladder listening to the end of the story. Then he brings the stepladder back inside.* **David** *slowly follows him in.*

Andy I think she got over ye, she was no shrinkin' . . . she was no stranger to . . . Caught on the Pax cam more than once. Mind you, ye haven't done too badly yourself, either, there's been a few young ones brought back here over the years, but only . . . not in the ha'penny . . . not like . . . the twinkle . . . ye had . . . in your eyes . . .

David When?

Andy The fuckin' twinkle be Jaysus and I . . . I knew . . .

David Knew what?

Andy I knew, well, you didn't let on, of course, not a word till I quizzed ye up.

David What are you . . .?

Andy Emma.

David What about her?

Andy Fuckin' Emma, the first weekend you mentioned her to me . . . lettin' on as if it was nothin', but I . . .

David You knew . . . by the twinkle . . .?

Andy In your fuckin' eyes, boy, I knew, so I prodded a bit, eventually gettin' the full Johnnymagorry outta ye. How ye's had met . . . all a that, and I knew, by the way ye spoke about her. I even, at home that night, I told Marie, We'll have him married yet. Then when I met her meself, she had such a lovely way about her. She seemed to be the kind of one . . . her singin', her whole, whadyemacallit, attitude . . . the kind of one who isn't afraid to take anythin' on, ye know? I just got that from her. You're lucky, Davy . . . to have someone like that.

Andy *takes the ladder through the auditorium doors. David moves to the box office and deposits the plastic letters inside the glass. Andy bursts back through the auditorium doors.*

Do ye know what we'll do when she arrives, do ye?

David   What'll we do?

Andy   Bring her inside and make her stand in front of the screen, and we'll sit in the middle row, and she'll . . . she can belt out an ol' song for us. We'll demand a song, and then we'll have an ol' drink, what do ye think?

David   We'll see how we go, Andy . . .

Andy   It'll be only her second night in the Savoy, but it'll be your last, has to be marked, isn't that right? It will bedad, it'll be a night never to be forgotten. It will be like the night I invited Marie to the dance in Dublin, a crowd of us used t' go in a bus, had a desperate job persuadin' the da, but he gave in eventually and she sat in beside me . . . lookin' great, she'd really made the effort . . . and so had I, moved around the . . . fuckin' glided around that dance floor, had got a few lessons from Jackie, put the rest of them to . . . A rose, I'd given her a red rose which she broke the stem of and put in her hair . . . Around that floor . . . Fred Astaire and Ginger Rogers . . . every eye on us. And later on, outside her house, with the da peekin' through the curtains at us . . . I asked her to . . . tie the . . . would she be my . . . That's the way it happened . . . Mr and Mrs Connolly. Maybe tonight when Emma arrives I'll fuck off home . . . leave the two of ye alone.

David   There's no need for that, Andy . . .

Andy   Ah now, I know that the last time ye were down I kinda hogged her a bit . . .

David   Well, sure, you were only tryin' to get to know her.

Andy   And I know that you were kinda thick with me.

David   I wasn't . . .

Andy   And I'll tell ye how I know that, because I was dyin' for us to do Clint for Emma, but all you wanted to do was leave rale quick.

David   Listen, Andy . . . me and Emma were . . . it wasn't you. We were fighting at the time, weren't the best . . .

Andy   Right . . . ah, Jesus God love ye, at each other's . . . Murder she wrote, was it . . .

David   Yeah, me and Emma were under a bit of strain. That was all.

Andy *is distracted by someone rattling one of the doors to see if it is open. Then there is a knock.* **Andy** *recognises who it is and goes to the door.*

Andy   It's the Penders . . .

Andy *has the door open and lets the couple in.* **David** *is agitated and retreats to his seat on the stairs.*

Andy   Podge, it's yourselves . . . I knew ye's would be over.

Podge   Good man, Andy.

Liz   How are ye, Andy?

Andy   How's Liz?

Podge   The last night, wha' . . . Hard to believe.

Andy   Ah, now, fuck a duck.

Liz   Well, we just had to come over . . .

Podge *produces a bottle wrapped in a brown-paper bag.*

Podge   To say how much we did always love comin' here, so . . .

Andy *takes it and unwraps part of the brown paper. It is a bottle of Power's.*

Podge   Where she snared me that first time.

Liz *gives him a playful punch.*

Andy   Ah, ye's are very good, honest to . . .

Liz   It's nothin' . . . for all the . . .

Podge   . . . the entertainment over the years . . . (*To* **David**.) How are ye?

Liz   How's it goin'? Liz Pender.

David   How are ye . . . David.

Liz   Ye probably wouldn't remember me. I was the year ahead of ye in school.

David   I know . . . Yeah, I recognise you.

Liz   Jeez . . . do ye?

David   I do.

Liz   And this is Podge . . .

Podge   Used t' work in your da's supermarket years ago, at the checkouts, every Saturday . . .

David   Oh, right.

Liz   We were laughin' in the pub, weren't we . . .

Podge   We were.

Liz   Earlier on.

Podge   A good ol' laugh.

Liz   I says, I says, do ye remember the time Andy wouldn't let me into see *Porky's* that time?

Podge   Never forget, says I, and we the only two in the town who didn't get to see it.

Liz Rage of the age it was.

Andy You were under-age, Liz.

Liz Eventually saw it on video anyways, it wasn't that great.

Podge I thought it was brilliant.

Andy Did it put ideas in his head, Liz?

Liz It did alright . . . in his head, and that's where they stayed.

Andy Don't believe ye . . . Here . . . here, stay for a . . . (*Holds up bottle.*)

Podge What do ye think, Liz?

Andy Come on, join the wake, come on, you being the great customers that ye were.

Liz Sure, I suppose we could, a small one to . . .

Podge . . . say goodbye to the place.

Andy Exactly. We've only the three cups so one of ye may take a nip out of the cap . . .

Podge The Power's, a nip, yeah . . .

Andy *opens up the bottle and hands it to* **Podge**, *who pours a drop into the cap.*

Andy *retrieves the cup Pax had been drinking from and hands it to* **Liz**.

Liz Thanks.

Podge *hands* **Liz** *the bottle and she pours herself a measure.*

Andy Want a drop, Davy?

Andy *notices* **David** *standing up a little unsteadily to proffer his cup.* **Andy** *takes the bottle from* **Liz** *and pours him a measure.*

Andy Are we right? Okay . . . To the Savoy and all her loyal customers!

They all drink.

Liz   Podge . . .

Podge   Wha . . . Oh yeah, we were . . . across in Mac's and, eh . . . Pax told us that yourself was here, so . . .

Liz (*to* **David**)   . . . that you were over here. Ye see, my mother is mad into the . . . the show . . .

Podge   So I says to Liz that if we go over across to Andy to say goodbye to the Savoy and we don't ask . . .

Liz   Like if we don't ask for an autograph, she'd be fierce vexed . . .

Podge   Like if she knew that we were over here with you and we hadn't . . .

Liz   . . . asked you, like, she'd be . . .

Podge   . . . fierce disappointed so . . .

He holds out a peeled beer-mat and a pen to **David**.

David   Right, no problem.

He takes the pen and beer-mat.

To who?

Liz   Me ma.

David   Does she have a name?

Liz   Oh, yeah . . . Ann.

David   To Ann.

He writes.

Podge   Pity about here . . . that ye couldn't have held on for a bit longer.

Liz   Yeah, right enough, until the meat factory opens.

Andy   Opening down the Tunnel Road, isn't it?

Podge   Yeah, three hundred jobs, people movin' to the town, a few more bob around.

Liz   Shame ye's couldn't have . . . Ah sure, every cloud has a silver linin' . . .

Podge   True . . . a factory opening is bread and butter whereas here is . . . not bein' impudent now, but here is just bricks and mortar and a bit of an ol' show, ye know . . .

Andy   Well Jaysus, talk about kickin' a fella at his own funeral . . .

Liz   Ah, ye know what we mean, Andy . . .

Andy   I suppose . . .

Podge   But still, like it is an awful pity about the place.

Andy   I suppose ye'll have to . . . to go to Tallaght now.

Podge   Oh yeah, right enough . . . won't be the same though.

Liz   Ah no, it just doesn't have the same . . .

Podge   Liz . . .

Liz   It'll never be the same as . . .

Andy   You've been up there?

Liz   We . . . now we just . . .

Podge   We . . . to be honest with ye, Andy, that's where we were tonight,.

Liz   Ye see, we'd seen *Ace Ventura* here last Sunday and . . . and . . .

Podge   And the new Bond came out this weekend so's and she's . . .

Liz   I'm mad into . . .

Podge   Was a fierce Remington Steele fan so's . . .

Liz   Mad to see himself . . .

Podge   Pierce . . . to see what he's like as . . .

Liz   . . . as . . . Bond, ye know . . . like if this place hadn't a been closin' we would have waited, wouldn't we?

Podge Of course . . .

Andy I suppose . . . ye's were always great customers and that's the truth, a few more like ye and we wouldn't be closin' at all . . .

David *has been watching the previous exchange, beer-mat in hand. He holds it out for* **Podge** *to take back.*

Podge I wonder, could ye ever . . . on the other side?

David *turns the mat around and starts to write on the other side.*

David Oh right . . . To Liz and Podge . . .

Podge Ah no . . . not us.

David What . . .

Liz No like, ah, we don't . . .

Podge We wouldn't . . . be particularly interested in . . .

Liz What he meant was . . . could ye sign the back of it to a Mrs Kelly . . .

Podge She'd love that, Mrs Kelly next door to us, she'd be delighted . . . 'Cause we don't really watch it, like . . .

Liz No, no . . . we think it's kinda . . .

Podge . . . shite.

Liz No offence.

David To Mrs Kelly. Best wishes.

He hands the beer-mat and pen back to **Podge**.

Podge Thanks a million.

Liz Thanks for that.

David Do you think that I'm shite in it?

Liz No, oh no . . . you're . . .

Podge Very good, you're very . . .

Liz One of the best in it.

David   How do ye know?

Podge   Pardon?

David   How do you know what I'm like if you never watch it?

Liz   Well, we don't really, but . . .

Podge   We've seen you in it. The whole town thinks you take a great part in it, don't they?

Liz   Oh yeah . . . Lord, yeah . . .

Podge   Whole town is fierce proud of ye, aren't they, Andy?

Andy   Well, if they're not they should fuckin' be, but of course this town is . . . can be . . . fierce contrary.

Liz   Ah, I think most people . . .

Podge   Yeah . . . yeah . . . delighted that he's . . . representin' the town, ye know, one of our own . . .

Andy   And don't forget a rake of other fellas would have applied for it.

Podge   I'd say.

Andy   A deluge, but our Davy got the part.

Liz   Tell us now, did ye always want to be an actor?

David   Yeah . . .

Podge   Ye'd never any interest in stayin' in the town, like, goin' into the supermarket with your da . . .?

David   No, no interest . . .

Podge   Just as well after he sellin' it on to Quinsworth, be Jaysus . . .

Liz   True . . . ah sure, anyways, good luck to ye . . . RTE today, Hollywood tomorrow.

Podge   Oh yeah, I mean ye'd have to be gettin' outta that shite at some stage . . .

Liz Podge!

Andy Hold on there, now . . . why do so many people watch it, then?

Liz True . . . just behind the *Late Late* in the ratings.

David *forces a smile and drains his mug. Very awkward silence. He fixes himself another drink.*

Podge I'd say you boys, all you boys on it, I'd say, ye's get some amount of women above in Dublin.

Liz Podge!

Podge I'm only . . . ye know, bein' on the telly and everythin'.

Andy He's settled on the one woman now, Podge.

Podge Is that right?

Andy Gorgeous young one, ye'd want to see her, lads, if he had any sense he'd . . . She's drivin' down to us tonight. Drivin' down for the wake . . . Peg out the photo, Davy . . .

David Ah Jesus, Andy . . .

Liz Show us . . .

Podge Do . . .

Andy Come on a mhic . . .

David Okay, Christ . . .

David *takes out photo and hands it to* **Liz**. *He moves to the doors, looking out to the square.*

Andy Isn't she . . .

Podge She is . . .

Liz Right enough . . . beautiful eyes . . .

Podge Beautiful pair a . . . eyes, alright.

Liz Podge!

Andy   She's a singer, like a fierce good singer, has her own band, be Jaysus, big concert above in . . . tonight, but she's due down . . . Could arrive at any . . . sorta, whadyecallit, Davy?

David   What . . .?

Andy   The type of singin'?

David   Blues . . .

Andy   Blues . . . jazzy . . . ye know.

Liz   She might do a concert in the town sometime? (*She hands* **David** *back the photo.*)

David   She might . . .

Andy   There does be photos of the two of them together, ye know, once in the *Evening Herald* and on the back of the *Sunday World.*

Liz   Go way . . . I'd hate that, though, the invasion of privacy and . . .

David   Jesus, it's not like we have the paparazzi camped out in the fucking garden.

Andy   One day ye will, Davy, huh, one day . . .

Liz   So . . . how long are yourself and herself . . .

Andy   Livin' together this six months, goin' out this year and a half, that right, Davy?

David   That's right.

Liz   Grand job . . . well good luck to ye's . . . We should head . . .

Podge   Thanks for the jar . . .

Liz   And the . . . (*She indicates the autographed beer-mat in her hand.*)

Andy   Good luck, lads.

Podge *and* **Liz** *make their way towards the doors.*

David   How long have you been together?

Podge   Us? Must be . . .

Liz   Well, I was in me last year in school.

David   And ye're happy?

Liz   We are.

Podge   Ah yeah, when she's not . . .

Liz *gives him a look.*

Podge   Yes . . . we're fierce happy.

David   I thought that . . .

Podge   We should . . .

Liz   Bye . . . bye now.

They turn towards the door.

Andy   See ya's, thanks for the bottle.

David   Tell us, how do you do it?

Podge   Excuse me?

Podge *and* **Liz** *glance at each other in a 'How the fuck do we get out of here?' way.*

David   You said that you met him when you were still in school and you're still standing here, however many years later, so how do you do it?

Podge *and* **Liz** *grin at each other, not knowing how to respond.*

David   Okay . . . okay, first things first . . . I remember you in sixth year goin' out with Dessie Denehan, so . . . like, when did you split up from him?

Liz   Well, ye have us rale . . . goin' red now . . .

Podge   She only went with Dessie a wet week . . .

David   Yeah . . .

Liz   Ah yeah . . . Dessie was an awful gob-shite. So when
I broke it off with him I . . . ye see, Podge, like, he was
fierce shy, so there was no way Jose that he was going to
ever make a move, and I was a bit the same, so my best
friend Audrey went up to him one Saturday in your da's
supermarket.

Podge   That's right . . .

Liz   So's she arranged him to meet me outside here the
following week. Lord, when I think of it, standin' outside
there like a gnoc, thinkin' that he'd never turn up . . .

Podge   I had to get a lift into the town from the brother
so I was . . .

Liz   Ten minutes, be Jaysus, I was waitin', and Andy, you
came out to me to say that the film was after startin'.

Andy   I did . . .

Liz   So's anyways, your man appears, all rale sorry and
nervous, with just about enough few bob for the tickets . . .
I think it was twenty-five or so pence in those days . . . that
be right, Andy?

Andy   Twenty-five . . .

Liz   We went up anyways, and there was no way I was
sittin' with him in the back row, first date like, so we sat up
in the front row, stiff as boards, watchin', it was a kids' yoke.

Podge   *Herbie Goes Bananas* . . .

Liz   Well, neither of us went bananas that night, when
I think of it, but we arranged to meet the next Friday over
beyond in the Copper Beach and the ol' slow dance and . . .

Podge *nudges her.*

Podge   We were away, huh . . .?

Liz   That was the last year in school and we got married
three years later . . .

Podge   Oh, cash and carried . . .

Liz   In the spring of '85 . . . got the house in St John's Road . . . a struggle in those times, but sure . . . it's ours now. Built an extension two or three year ago . . .

David   Have you kids?

Liz   Jeez, it's like bein' on whadyecallit, *This is Your Life*. We have, Patrick and Linda.

Podge   Keep ye on your toes . . .

Liz   So that's us . . .

David   But how have you kept it together for so long?

Liz   Us? Ye just . . . get on with it . . . and sure it helps when you're still very fond of each other. That's right . . .

Liz *puts her arm around* **Podge***'s waist.*

Liz (*indicating* **Andy**)   Sure, this man will tell ye, how long are you and Marie now . . .

Andy   Forty year, last October.

Liz   Ups and downs, but when ye decide on someone . . . isn't that right, Andy?

Andy *nods, and lights a smoke.*

David   Surely though, there must have been a time when you got . . . bored with each other?

Podge   We'll really have to go . . .

Liz   Look, you were very good to sign the thing, but we have to . . .

David   I mean, you must have had your eye on other people?

Podge   No, no, we never did. Goodnight, Andy . . .

They try a few of the doors to see which one is open.

David   I mean, do you sometimes wake up in the morning and turn around and see the other one asleep and wish that you were . . .? I mean, has either one of you ever slept with anyone else? I mean, surely in all that time one of you must have wanted to . . .?

Podge   Is he jarred?

Liz   Listen here, now . . .

David   I'm sorry, it's just, I'm only asking. Ye see, Emma, my girl, the . . . in the photo . . . lately I . . . I don't think she's being completely honest . . . Ye see, I think there's another guy . . . this friend of hers . . . he always seems to be around and I've been watching them . . .

Andy   Ah, come on, be Jaysus, a friend is a friend . . .

David   No . . . the other week . . . he came back to our place and there was a, ye know . . . a . . . between them. You know, the way you can just feel a thing . . .

Andy   Come on now, are ye jumpin' to . . . be Jaysus, ye are . . .

David   I know what I felt that night . . . The funny thing is, what's really funny, is that they suit each other . . . into the same stuff, music, all of that.

Podge   Andy, could ye . . . which fuckin' door is it?

Andy *does not move to assist* **Podge** *and* **Liz***'s escape.*

Andy   Out of your . . . get all that out of your ceann. She'll be down here tonight, nowhere else or with no one . . .

David   I want what you have . . .

Andy   What I have?

David   I want to be with someone for forty years and still be willing to do what you do for Marie . . . the way you take care of her is . . . and the two of you are . . . are brilliant to be . . . since school. That's so . . . it was good to meet you both.

Liz   Well, of course it must be fierce difficult for the likes of ye . . .

David   Pardon . . .

Podge *has finally managed to open the right door.*

Podge   Come on, Liz . . .

Liz   Yourself and the young one . . . showbiz. I don't know, ye read about it all the time, sure yous are always hoppin' around . . .

Podge   Liz . . .

Liz   I'm only tryin' to say like . . . the sense of . . . the rale world, everyday things that would keep the likes of us . . . grounded, but the like of ye wouldn't have . . . ye know . . .

David   You haven't a fucking clue . . .

Liz   Sometimes, maybe, you people, head does be in the clouds . . .

Podge   For the lord lamb of jeez will ye come on, Liz?

Liz   I'm sayin' nothin' . . . I'm only sayin' that it must be more difficult for ye to knuckle down, ye know? In a relationship, there always has to be a bit of . . .

David   Hold on . . . what are you talking about? . . . I just think that my girlfriend may be interested in someone else . . .

Liz   That's what I mean, the likes of ye . . . always hoppin' around . . .

David   The likes of . . . What the fuck are you . . .? The likes of me . . .? No, you're right . . . the likes of me, because at least the likes of me has had a bit of experience away from here.

Pax   What's wrong with here?

David   There's nothing . . . nothing wrong with here . . .

Podge   We'll head off to fuck, Andy.

David   I'm just saying that if ye'd . . . Given different circumstances, Liz . . . or you, Podge . . . ye wouldn't be averse to . . . with someone else, but no, ye'd never chance anything . . . afraid that, God forbid, ye might lose it all and end up on your own. So you just stick it, no matter what . . . you'll always just stick it out . . .

Liz   You'd want to sober . . .

David   Or is it the plain fact that nobody else would fucking look at either one of you?

Podge   Are you lookin' for a fuckin' box, are ye?

Podge *goes for* **David**, *pushing him back.*

Andy   Ah, Podge, he's . . . Don't mind . . .

Podge   Think ye can talk to us like that? Maybe ye could when you people owned half the town, well that day is over, everyone knows that your da is strugglin'.

Liz   Come on . . . Podge, come on, he's not worth . . .

Podge   The fuckin' Roller hasn't been seen in a while, ye see, we're not thick, we notice these things.

David   I'll fucking talk to you any way I like, it has nothing to do with my father or how much of this fucking town we ever owned . . .

Podge *goes for him again.* **Andy** *gets in the way.*

Andy   Podge, leave it now, leave it now . . .

Podge   I'll fuckin' bury him . . .

Liz   Podge, come on, stop it . . .

Andy   Christ, Davy, will ye fuck off inside there, go way . . . Podge . . . calm it down there . . .

David *walks unsteadily up the stairs.*

Podge   Bollocks . . .

Andy   Just get the fuck out, will ye . . .

Liz   Come on now, we're goin' . . .

Podge *isn't moving.* **Liz** *has a hold of his arm. He relents and follows her to the door, which* **Andy** *is holding open.*

Andy   Could ye blame a chap, people come here . . . sayin' what ye do is . . . shite, but still wantin' names on beer-mats for . . . go on, now.

Podge   Do ye know somethin' about Tallaght, Andy . . .?

Andy   Wha about fuckin' Tallaght?

Podge   Apart from the better seats . . . sound, screen, fuckin' proper popcorn . . .

Andy   Fuckin' Tallaght . . .

Podge   The best thing is that there'll be no more of you sittin' on that stool, makin' ol' . . .

Liz   Podge . . .

Podge   . . . stupid remarks, embarrassin' her . . . the big laugh, we'd all join in, but dyin' for to get away inside . . .

Andy *is too stunned to speak.*

Podge   Yeah, that'll be the best thing . . . that we'll never have to listen to your ol' shite while we're tryin' to buy our tickets.

Podge *turns and is gone out of the door before* **Andy** *can react. He is clearly hurt.*

Liz (*in a small voice*)   See ya, Andy.

Liz *leaves.* **Andy** *takes a moment to survey the empty foyer and then goes over and takes down the* ACE VENTURA *poster, followed by the home-made* NOW SHOWING *card above it. He goes back to his stool and sits.*

Lights down. Curtain.

Act Two

Film score music during blackout begins to swell as lights fade up on cinema curtains, which open to reveal the cinema screen. We are now inside the auditorium. **David** *stands on stage in front of the curtain and screen. The theatre where the play is being performed is now the empty cinema auditorium.* **Andy** *enters through the door at the back of the theatre/cinema auditorium. Carrying a pile of posters under one arm, he begins to walk down the aisle, shining his torch under the rows of seats to check for anything that might have been left behind. Music fades out.*

Andy Ne'er a thing . . . so few here, sure . . . (*Up to* **David**.) Alright?

David Alright . . .

Andy Jarred?

David No . . . Yeah . . . sorta . . .

Andy Thought that . . .

David I started . . . earlier than I usually . . . a bar beside busaras . . . lunchtime.

Andy Ah, Davy . . .

David When I got down here off the bus, across in the house, I made the effort for you, to be . . . ye know . . . wasn't goin' to take another drink . . . but . . .

Andy Be Jaysus, drinkin' since . . . ah . . .

David It was just, sitting in that house, expecting Dad to phone . . . he was supposed to have, just this fucking once, made the effort to . . .

Andy But you said he did, you said he . . .

David Well, he didn't. So I was annoyed. Of course I'll never let him know that I was annoyed . . . we're always so civil to each other . . . Jesus, I can't fucking believe that I started going off like that to those people.

Andy   Ah, don't mind them, fuckin' gnocs at the end of the day . . . They haven't the first clue about . . . just 'cause they don't like the show . . .

Andy *is now in front of the screen and sets the pile of posters down.*

David   No . . . they're nice people, Andy. Did ye see them? They're together . . . they're . . . they're right about the . . . I don't like the fucking thing . . . I don't . . . but then I . . . Jesus, I'm lucky to be in it . . .

Andy   They're lucky to have you . . .

David   I've slipped into this . . . liking the fact of being . . . on the street, a group of teenage girls giggle after me or a group of old women point and whisper, and I . . .

Andy   Why wouldn't ye like it, a mhic . . . young ones givin' ye the eye . . . sure we'd all . . . makin' the cover of the *RTE Guide* that time . . .

David   I know, it's ridiculous. I got such a thrill out of that. I still get such a thrill out of being recognised, or if someone does take our picture for the poxy *Herald* . . . and I know it's ridiculous. Anyway, anyway, it doesn't matter . . . it doesn't matter any more . . . it's not going to be a fucking problem any more . . .

Andy   What do ye mean?

David   I was called in to the office yesterday.

Andy   The office . . .?

David   The office, the producer's . . .

Andy   The show . . .

David   Yes . . . I've been late and not knowing lines and generally been a pain in the hole, they've put up with it for a while, but last week I came in drunk . . .

Andy   Ah, Davy.

David   Them talking about fucking counsellors . . . I got thick . . . did the 'You can stick your job up your hole', walked out feeling great . . . for ten minutes. Oh fuck it . . .

Andy   Davy . . . no . . . locked in the mornin' time . . .

David   So I've quit . . .

Andy   Christ and they . . . let ye, just like that? Mistake, they've made a big . . .

David   No they haven't . . . I was out of it, didn't know lines . . . wasn't fit to work . . . Jesus, I'd come in to work pissed . . . the night before, me and Emma had the biggest row of our lives.

Andy   Over?

David   What?

Andy   The row . . . over?

David   We'd all been out, in a nightclub, and . . .

Andy   Was it over . . . your man . . . this other fella?

David   No . . .

Andy   Surely she's not . . .

David   I don't know.

Andy   Surely she's not . . .

David   It was just a feeling that I got that night.

Andy   That the two of them were . . .

David   Yes, but . . . the night of the row he wasn't around, so it was . . . we were all having a good time, a group of us, mostly her friends, and I had found myself talking about this place, how much it meant to me growing up and how I'd miss it, telling stories, ye know, like what we've been at tonight. But Emma, out of the blue . . . starts to say, she's pretty bolloxed, but she starts saying how I don't really feel what I say I do about this place, that I put it on. A big phoney, sentimental Savoy Paradiso act that I put on to impress people, and that when the Savoy closes down it won't really matter to me, not really, it won't impact on my life like it will on . . . and then she mentioned your name.

Andy Me. She mentioned me?

David She did . . . Andy's life, she said . . . sayin' that when the Savoy closes that I won't bother ever trying to see you and you'll be lost, stuck at home with a wife who barely speaks . . .

Andy How . . . She doesn't . . . know me . . . has no fuckin' business . . .

David Look it, Andy . . . She was just trying to get at me, and . . .

Andy Christ Almighty, when she arrives down here tonight I'll put her straight on a few things . . . about us . . . tell her about . . . I mean, did you not tell her about the matinee, you creelin' yourself, twisted ankle be Jaysus, after *Fistful of Dollars*, me cartin' ye across to the house but your da wasn't home yet, and so there was nothin' for it only to bring ye up to my house . . . Did ye not tell her . . .?

David Yeah . . . yes, I did . . . I told her . . .

Andy And us chattin' non-stop about the films . . . in my front room, and you on about school . . . Jimbob Hickey havin' a go at ye but you took him on . . . saw him off . . . You said you saw him off like Clint would have, I did have to laugh . . . like Clint . . .

David Gave him a fistful . . .

Andy A fistful . . . Jimbob sittin' on top of ye, tryin' to be the big man . . . but you showed him, Davy.

David I fucking did, he never went near me again . . . so I told her all this.

Andy How ye came up to mine every Saturday, after that?

David I told her . . . every Saturday after the matinee.

Andy Good man, Davy . . . like we always said, a mhic . . . we'll never . . .

David . . . lose touch, never. I told her . . . Savoy or no Savoy, we'll never . . .

Andy   Good man, Davy . . .

David   It's great to be here . . . I was really looking forward to coming down here, to be . . . thinking of those matinees . . . years ago, sitting out there, and whatever was botherin' you as a kid, you'd just look up at that big screen and whatever it was would just disappear, you'd feel nothing but comfort, nothing but good . . . ye know . . . safe . . .

Andy   That Saturday too, I'll never forget, leavin' ye back to your da . . . the front door shuttin' and you runnin' to the window to wave me goodbye. Felt kinda . . . whadyema-callit . . . lonely for ye, a little fella with no ma. I walked back over here for the night show, but happy too 'cause I felt that I'd been a . . . as ye say . . . comfort . . .

David   You were, you and Marie . . . Marie . . . she . . . she had this thing about getting kisses from me, if she produced a sweet or a miwadi orange . . . and I would, I'd kiss her on the cheek, and the funny thing was that I was sure that you were jealous because your face . . . kind of sour or something, whenever she was trying to get the kiss out of me . . . And then you'd whisk me away to the front room and we'd listen to the spaghetti western soundtrack . . .

Andy   Absolutely brilliant . . .

David   I liked the way the two of ye's seemed to . . . a tug of war to get my attention . . . centre of attention in your house . . . not like . . . Sure, Dad could barely look me in the eye.

Andy   Can't have been easy for him . . . losin' your mother so young.

David   I know . . . I was the image of her . . . everyone said.

Andy   Ye were . . . still are . . .

David   He's . . . selling the house. He's going to live in London, full time . . . so I mightn't be down here too often from now on . . .

Andy   Sellin' the . . . jeanny . . . but there's no reason for
ye not to, there's a, be Jaysus, spare room, waitin' for ye . . .
any time ye like, a mhic . . . up above in my house . . .
Christ, it'll be like, wha' . . . you and me . . . Morricone full
blast in the living room. Ye can bring down herself . . . wha',
there's a big enough bed there . . . wha' . . . wha' . . .

David   Maybe we could, Andy . . .

Andy   Oh yeah, tonight when she walks through the front
doors, all the falling out will be forgotten, ye'll put it all
behind ye's . . . (*Clapping his hands.*) Come on, a mhic, time is
marchin', let's get this wake goin' again, wha'? What do ye
say? Anyways, you'll be up there one day, up on that screen,
wha' . . . Fuck the telly . . . your dream, be Jaysus, I know
well, since ye were a gassoon . . . do ye know . . . we'll
fuckin' reopen . . . when your film comes out, your da will
have money again and we'll fuckin' reopen the place, a
premiere here . . . wha', in the Savoy, wha' . . . yourself and
Emma on a . . . walkin' on a . . . red . . . crowds in the
square . . . carpet, be Jaysus . . . Podge and the Missus will
be sorry they didn't take your name with them then . . .

He leans down and takes up a plastic bag.

Andy   Christ, I nearly . . . it nearly slipped me . . . Davy,
I have this for ye . . . just to mark the . . . (*He takes a framed
picture out of the bag.*) Meant to give it to ye earlier but ye
know yourself with all the distractions and that . . .

David   Thanks, that's . . . that'll go straight up on my wall.

David *goes over and gives* **Andy** *a hug. We see the framed picture is
a photo of himself and Andy outside the Savoy.*

Andy   It's one the *Leinster Express* took of the two of us, that
time in '83, at the openin', when we'd done the revamp . . .
new seats and all that . . . remember?

David   *Tootsie* . . .

Andy   Good man, right ye be . . . We showed *Tootsie*, good
show . . . Jeez, we better sort through those posters, 'cause

there's a few good ones, like, a lotta shite, but . . . ye'd never know what ye'd find.

Andy *gives* **David** *a wink and goes over to the pile of posters that he's brought in. They begin to sort through them.* **Pax** *suddenly enters the auditorium.*

Pax   LADS! Here's ye are . . . Guess what! . . . Lads . . .

Andy   Ah, here he is . . .

David   How's Pax . . .?

Pax   Right, right . . . Lads, lads, lads . . . guess what . . . here, here . . . take up yer cups . . . take them up.

They do what they're told and **Pax** *starts to pour them whiskey from an already opened bottle he's brought in.*

Pax   Ye won't believe what . . . Willy Muirin stood up, cleared his ol' throat, be gorra mighty, and announced that he was steppin' down, which we were all kinda expectin' as the health wasn't the Mae West. So's . . . so's . . . doesn't Mucky Meehan nominate me, the Mouse seconds it, I was up with a chance . . . all of a sudden I was in with a shout. The Body Brennan nominates Noelly MacNally and the Badger seconds him, so's it's the two of us, a vote . . . there and then, a vote. Guess what . . . guess fuckin' what? I was elected, can ye . . .? They elected me . . . me . . . Well, lads, I nearly choked, and that's no coddin' or jokin', had to make a speech and everythin', how I'd do me best for the club, give it me all, that'd be a big responsibility, but as Rory Smullen said to me afterwards, 'Who knows the club better than you, Pax?' he said, and he's right when I think of it, no one knows that soccer club better than I do. Ah, here lads, drink up, drink up with me . . .

There is a slight pause as **Pax** *presumes one of them will toast his success.* **David** *finally raises his cup.*

David   Congratulations, Pax. To . . . the . . . new president!

Pax   Thanks, thanks . . . I mean, I suppose in me heart and soul, as the fella says, I did think that Willy would step down, a good man, a great servant to the . . . but, ye know, gettin' a bit doddery, forgettin' things . . . Thanks, lads . . . I was that excited I nearly forgot about ye's . . .

Andy In your hour of glory . . .

Pax In me . . . I nearly did . . .

Andy Everyone clappin' ye on the back . . .

Pax Christ, yeah, nearly did . . .

Andy Nearly forgot about your watch as well, did ye, Pax?

Pax The fuckin' . . . the watch, nearly did . . .

David Well, it's only to be expected . . . elected to the top job . . .

Pax People was very generous is all I'll say . . . the porter was flowin', the Mouse had his guitar out, but I thought of ye and this place . . .

David You were very good to come back across, Pax.

Pax Not at all . . . It is the . . . had to come over and tell ye's . . . I was thinkin' it's funny, 'cause even if the pictures wasn't closin' at all I would have had to quit anyways, 'cause of bein' elected. I would have had to leave me evenin's free for the club meetin's and a rake of organisin' and that, would have had to quit anyhow. Funny, that . . .

Andy Noelly MacNally ye say was the other . . . the other candidate, ye say . . . They must have been . . . Sure, Noelly can barely spell his own name. Is that the best they could come up with?

Pax Excuse me . . . Noelly . . . Noelly's fierce popular in that club, a great man for the fund-raisers, great craic in him.

Andy The brightest star in the fuckin' cosmos . . .

Pax Don't mind . . . David, don't mind that fella . . . Noelly . . . Did ye ever hear about Noelly when he was workin' above in the granary, always late, almost every

mornin', a guarantee . . . Noelly shamblin' up the yard, five
or ten past, ye could set your watch by him . . . One
mornin' doesn't Tommy Welsh come out of his office and
spots him. 'Late again, Noelly,' says Welsh to him, 'Like
meself, Mister Welsh,' says Noelly, 'like meself,' and strolls
on up the yard. Well, we did laugh when we heard that . . .

David (*laughing*)   'Like meself, Mister Welsh . . .'

Pax   Honest to . . . David . . . Gas but . . . by Jaysus, we're
goin' to absolutely malavogue pints of porter over there
tonight.

Andy   The soccer club, this is all I'll say, it must be in
some state if the only two gnocs up for . . . was you and the
laziest, good for nothin', wouldn't-organise-a-ride-in-a-brothel
fuckin' Noelly MacNally . . .

David   Ah, come on, Andy, credit where credit is . . .

Pax   Well, be the fuckin' hoakies, do you know somethin'?

Andy   It's . . . nobody else was . . . could be arsed enough
to go for the stupid . . .

Pax   Andy Connolly, you are the greatest begrudgin'
bollocks that this town has ever seen . . .

Andy   They nominated the two of ye 'cause . . .

Pax   'Cause why? 'Cause why? How would you know what
way the soccer club is . . .?

Andy   . . . 'cause they knew ye'd be the only fools willin'
to do it.

Pax   How would you know, huh . . .? Were ye ever at a
meetin'?

Andy   I know by the crowd that's in it . . . a right shower.

Pax   The crowd that's . . . You don't know them.

Andy   I know all about them . . . some committee you
have . . . the Badger Fennelly, never been off the dole in his
life. Mouse Mahr . . . over forty years of age and still livin'

with his mother. The Body Brennan . . . Christ, Davy, the high stool, all day, every day. And last but not . . . Mucky Meehan . . . least . . . some man . . . the whole of my road knows that he's been slappin' around the wife for years. Some shower . . .

Pax   Ye have the low-down on everyone . . . so what about me . . . what sort am I . . .?

Andy   You're a . . .

David   Would you both stop . . . for a second just . . .

Pax   Wouldn't say it to me face, wouldn't be your style . . .

Andy   You're a . . .

David   Fuck's sake . . .

Pax   And what are you? . . . What are you goin' to . . . I'll say it to ye now as it's the last night that I'll ever have to work with ye, I'll say it. What in the name of Jaysus are you goin' to do with yourself now, now this place is gone? Shut yourself away with Marie, in that house . . .?

Andy   Why don't you just shut your fuckin' . . . or I'll shut it for ye . . .

David   Lads. Come on . . . Jesus . . . men, please, stop . . .

Pax   Ye'd shut nothin' . . .

David   Have a drink, would ye's . . .

David *takes up the bottle and stands between them.*

David   The two of yous . . . A truce . . . please . . . Have a drink.

David *pours from the bottle into* **Andy**'s *cup.* **Pax** *turns away, drains his glass and heads towards the exit.*

David   Pax, where are you . . .? Pax, come on back . . .

Pax   I've enough of that . . . of that fella. I'm . . . I probably won't see much of ye's from now on . . .

David   Pax . . .

Andy   What about the watch . . . come on, the three of us, we'll pull the bastard projection room asunder till we find it.

Pax   It doesn't . . . it doesn't matter about the . . .

Andy   You're some . . . The watch, is it . . . Do ye know where that watch is . . . (*To* **David**.) 'Cause I know you know where it is, Pax.

Pax   How would I, how would . . . Why in the name of the good Lord fuck would I be searchin' if I knew . . .?

Andy   You know well.

Pax   I do, do I?

Andy   You do . . . At home, that's where it is . . . wherever ye keep it at home, at home . . . in your . . . in your own house.

Pax   In me own house . . .

Andy   Exactly, 'cause there was never a watch lost here . . .

Pax   I'm a liar now, am I?

Andy   There was somethin' else lost alright, but it wasn't a watch.

Pax   Callin' me a . . .?

Andy   The watch was only made up 'cause I seen ye pokin' around . . .

Pax   Do ye hear this?

Andy   For what ye really lost . . .

Pax   What is he . . .?

Andy *walks to the front of the stage and lifts up an edge of carpet.*

Andy   . . . or misplaced . . . (*He lifts up a loose bit of floorboard.*) It's a fierce pain in the Nat King Cole when ye leave somethin' somewhere and you go back the next day and it's vamoosed . . . a fierce browner, isn't it, Pax . . .?

Andy *takes a tin box from underneath the floorboard.*

David   What is it?

Andy   I stumbled across this a couple of months ago above in the projection box . . . Never let on, but I knew, I knew well that he'd be tryin' to snake it home tonight, so I moved it on him, for the . . . to brown him.

Pax   You're some . . .

Andy   Do ye want to have a look inside . . . do ye, ye'll get a laugh and that's the truth . . . a grown man with kids . . . Lord save us.

Pax *begins to walk back towards them.*

Pax   Give that over to me now, you.

Andy   Open it up, it's harmless enough, a class of a collection isn't it, Pax . . .?

Pax   Don't fuckin' touch it now, joke's over . . .

Andy   Come on, David, take it, open it up . . . take it, a mhic . . .

Pax   Leave it . . . give it over, Andy. Good joke, a great laugh, now hand it to me.

Andy   Here, I'll take the lid off for ye.

Andy *has the lid half-off and is handing the box to* **David**. **Pax** *piles in to grab it back.* **David** *lets go.* **Andy** *and* **Pax** *struggle for control of the box.*

Pax   Give . . . me the . . . fuckin' . . . thing . . .

Andy   No . . . fuckin' way . . . Jose . . .

The box slips from both their grasps and falls. Hundreds of individual film frames burst out of it and all over the floor. Nobody moves, until **David** *bends down and picks up some of the frames, holding them up to the light.*

Andy   A grown man, be Jaysus.

Pax   Have ye're laugh or whatever it is ye want.

David   Are they all . . . of the same thing?

Andy   Think so, the same thing . . . different shapes and sizes but basically the same thing.

David   And what . . . ye spliced a frame out of . . .

Andy   Like a, I don't know . . . a gassoon, a young fella who's never seen the real thing.

David   Impressive collection, Pax.

Andy   So that's what ye were doin' above in the projection box all these years . . . Makes sense now, when I do look back, ye could nearly always tell if there was a good tit-and-fanny film on, your man here would never leave the projection box . . .

Pax   Would you ever . . . What's the harm in lookin' up at a bit tit . . . It's a . . . it's as natural as . . .

David   Cutting frames of them out and keeping them in a tin box?

Pax   Look, I . . . honest to . . . I'm bein' honest with ye's now . . . One of the nights we were showin' some class of an English thing about a night nurse and like the reel broke during a sexy bit . . . and I was cuttin' and splicin' for to get the yoke back on, and I was left with a frame of this young blondie one, topless, gorgeous she was, so I . . . kinda kept her . . . and then I suppose I got into the habit of it . . . cuttin' and keepin' them . . . So there ye's have it . . . there in front of ye's.

Andy   Rita . . . If Rita . . . she'd do more then skin ye if she knew, although of course in fairness I'd hold her partly responsible, drivin' a grown man to collect women in a box. Of course she rules the roost, wears the . . . in that house. She must have left him to his own devices this long time . . .

Pax   Watch yourself now, Andy . . .

Andy   Mustn't a' been much action at home for ye like . . .

Pax Shut up . . .

Andy I'm sayin' nothin'.

Pax What am I? . . . Standin' here . . . listenin' to you . . .

He turns to go.

Andy Do ye not want to bring your women with ye . . .

Pax NO!!

Andy Well, ye better get home so, see will Rita grant you permission to take up your new post. That's the one thing ye don't want to end up doin', Davy, bein' fuckin' . . . ye know, under the big thumb, so goodnight . . . day, day . . . big thumb . . . ha . . . that's all I have to say . . . to you.

Pax *stops at the exit and slowly turns around.*

Pax By Jaysus . . . a thing starts, I dunno and ye say to yourself, none of my business . . . the odd time itchin' to . . . say somethin' to someone . . .

Andy Aaarahh, would ye ever go . . .

Pax Bringin' Rita into it . . .

Andy Why shouldn't I bring her into it, her sittin' at home every night and you here with your other women . . . huh, Davy. (*He laughs.*) His other women . . .

Pax She's not at home tonight, she's across the square in Mac's, celebratin' with me, proud of me . . . Where's your wife tonight, Andy . . .? Where is she . . .?

David Ah, come on now, Pax, he was only slaggin' ye . . .

Pax No, ye see your . . . if it was only slaggin' . . . it would only be slaggin' . . . but ye see he never quite forgave me . . .

Andy What are ye . . .?

Pax There was plenty he had his eye on, but Rita was number one, the best-lookin' one. Not that he ever even had the gumption to ask her or any of them out.

Andy   Thought you were goin' . . .

Pax   Like we'd all go off for the evenin' to a dance in Dublin, all dickied up, and ye had to be quick or the Dublin lads would be in before ye, there was no time for . . . fartin' about . . . and where was this man? Nowhere . . . never budgin' an inch all night, nursin' a Coke . . .

Andy   I never went in for all that . . .

David   Except for the night you and Marie, Fred Astaire and Ginger Rogers, the rose in her hair . . .

Pax   Not at all . . . What has he been . . . He never went near the floor . . . Big thick, not lettin' on to be head on him until it was time for the bus home, then not a word to any of us 'cause he hadn't been part of the craic, stoppin' for the chips in The Gem in Naas but he'd stay on the bus, sat up behind Dan Foran the driver, talkin' ol'-man talk to him 'cause he hadn't risked it . . .

Andy   Listen a mhic . . .

Pax   Put himself out there . . .

David   No, fuck this . . . this is . . . I know this man . . . He took Marie to that dance one night and afterwards he asked her to marry him. Didn't ye, Andy . . .?

Pax   Ye think ye know this man, maybe ye do . . . mind you, ye haven't been down much lately . . . sure you haven't been down here this six or seven months . . .

David   I've been . . .

Andy   . . . busy, he's been up to his . . .

Pax   Ah, before ye got on the telly, well before that be Jaysus, this last two or three year, ye've not been down as much . . . promisin' appearances that never materialised . . .

Andy   Come on, Davy . . . We'll leave this fucker to his own devices . . .

Pax   Then he was, all behind me back, when me and Rita started courtin'.

Andy Come on, a mhic . . .

Pax He was all how I was a snaky this and a egot that, and on our weddin' day . . .

Andy *tries to catch hold of* **David***'s arm.*

David Would ye hold on . . .

Pax Standin' with Rita and me outside the church, big handshake, kiss on the cheek for her, 'Congratulations to the both of ye's. I hope ye's will be very happy.' Christ, that must have stuck in your throat . . .

Andy I didn't give a flyin' . . . sure, didn't I have Marie?

Pax Ye did . . . poor Marie standin' there behind us, lookin' on.

Andy Me and Marie were fine . . .

Pax Ye's always seemed fierce odd to me.

David Odd . . .?

Pax Yeah . . . ye see in those days, Rita and Marie were great pals, so the four of us would be goin' out a lot, pub or functions and that, and I never once saw him . . . givin' her a hug . . . or givin' her a . . . an ol' kiss, nothin' like that.

Andy Well, ye see, Davy . . . Marie was fierce shy and she didn't . . .

Pax Shy nothin' . . . tryin' t' to slip her hand into your hand . . . Sittin' beside ye's . . . I could see it, she dyin' for ye to . . . and then the . . . I'd hear ye, all outta the side of your mouth, the comments on her hair, her dress . . . little put-downs . . .

Andy Aaaarahh . . .

Pax Her sittin', sippin' on her Madison, waitin' for ye to ask her out on the floor, always waitin' . . . And then the night I had the injured leg from the soccer, so's he, bein' the rale gentleman, asks Rita out, the one time he gets up, it's for Rita, and Marie there puttin' on the brave face, me

there tryin' to make chat. And then ye did ask her up for
the next dance but Marie knew well that it was Rita who'd
made ye . . . cryin' in the jacks later on. Rita found her in
the cubicle, pretendin' that she wasn't feelin' the Mae West,
and Rita was all on for sayin' somethin' to ye, but I told her
not to, that was the way in them days . . . ye never interfered
with a man's business, especially not his marriage . . . so
Rita thinks, boost her up, invites her to join the Boyne
Players, and Marie was kinda tickled by the idea, just
needed a bit of, ye know, geein' up, but oh no, the bold
Andy came out with just the right thing to put her off . . .
Sure why do ye think we stopped hangin' round ye? Couldn't
stick it . . .

Andy   All I said was that I didn't think that it would suit
her, that she wasn't the type to be . . .

David   To be what?

Andy   To be paradin' herself . . .

David   What do ye mean . .?

Andy   Well, Davy . . . all I said was . . . the likes of Marie
was put on the earth to . . . to . . . for to nest . . . cook . . .
keep the . . . clean . . . whilst women like Rita, on this earth
for to be looked at . . . doin' . . . admired . . . that's all
I said . . . didn't want her to be makin' a show of herself . . .

Pax   Why's that now, 'cause ye cared or somethin' . . .?

Andy   Didn't I ask her to marry me . . .?

Pax   And why did ye do that?

Andy   'Cause we'd . . . for fuck's sake, we'd talked about it,
we were . . . ready . . . whatever . . .

Pax   You never wanted her in the first place.

Andy   What is he . . .?

Pax   It was her approached you, on the bus, she left us to
sit up beside you in the front, never had the guts to choose
anyone yourself so you took her . . . ye married her . . .

Andy I don't fuckin' . . . throwin' shite at me, you . . . of all people. Can't believe we're listenin' to this gnoc . . . fella who . . . who gets off watchin' couples in the back row, fella who . . . his flute out in the projection box, this . . . this Rosie Dixon night-nurse fella . . .

Pax Do ye want me to go over and get Rita, she'll say it out straight?

Andy Do, do, we'll show her these while she's here . . . (*Indicates film frames scattered on the floor.*)

Pax Ye see those . . . be Jaysus . . . they're outta films, do ye get me? Just fuckin' pictures, they don't breathe or feel anythin' or . . . get hurt . . . see. They're not real, I just look at them, get me horn, does no one any harm, but what he's done . . . this fella . . .

Andy I can't . . . I have to . . . dread me ears for havin' to . . . come on . . . David, we've them posters to sort out, we've to, I'm not . . . Davy . . . a mhic . . .

Andy *moves to the exit.* **David** *stands still.*

Pax Rita'll tell ye . . . standin' outside the house that evenin' with Marie, waitin' for him to come home from this place . . .

Andy A mhic . . .

David *still isn't moving.* **Andy** *hesitates at the exit, but without David he can't leave.*

Pax She could hardly talk to her, to Rita, who used t' be her best pal . . . Rita tryin' to bring up the old days, the dances, comin' here to the pictures, the craic . . . but nothin' . . . tryin' to get her across to our house for a cup of tae, but there was no budgin' her out of that front gate . . .

Andy I know . . . haven't I fuckin' . . . lived with it for long enough, don't I be at home every night to tuck her in, say her prayers with her?

Pax And how do ye think she got into that state? Whittlin' away at her like that, be Jaysus for years, until she was . . .

Andy   Where is he gettin', all this pourin' out of him . . .?

Pax   Ah look, for years, be Jaysus, me trap shut for years, but sometimes a thing has to be said . . .

Andy   Has to be said . . . has to be . . . and of course all in front of Davy . . . that's what ye're up to. Can't ye see . . . he's . . . he's, I made a show of him with the box, back agin wall, so he's . . .

David   He's accusing you of treating your wife like a . . .

Andy   Unbelievable, isn't it? . . . Isn't it?

David   So why would he say it then . . .?

Pax   I'm saying it for Marie . . . her. The way he treated her.

Andy   He's only out to shame me . . .

Pax   Ah, here, I said what had to be said, take it whatever way ye's . . .

Andy   Forget all his . . . the last night be Jaysus . . . and we still . . . the posters to be sorted out . . .

Pax   Look it, there's a way a thing happened and ye can pretend all ye like that it didn't . . .

Andy   STAY FUCKIN' QUIET, YOU . . .

Andy *suddenly takes up the bottle of whiskey as if to fire it towards* **Pax**, *anything to get him to shut his mouth.*

Andy   GET OUT, WILL YE!

David *grabs hold of* **Andy** *before he can do any damage.*

David   Go on, Pax . . .

Andy   Tryin' to spoil . . .

Pax   I was only . . . I'm . . .

Andy   Ruinin' our last night . . .

David   Go on . . .

Pax   I . . . I'm sorry . . . I . . . but I'm glad ye know, God forgive me. I'm glad ye know what sort he is . . .

Andy *breaks away from* **David**, *and makes a drunken lunge for* **Pax**.

Andy   Cuuunnnnt!!!!

Pax *easily shoves him back.* **Andy** *does not try again. He turns away from them.*

Andy   Cunt . . .

David   Go on . . . go on, Pax . . .

Andy (*almost to himself*)   He's nothin' but a . . .

Pax   Nothin' but a . . . what . . .? I'll go back over to my wife, we'll have our drink, we'll walk home and we'll get in under the sheets together . . . We'll cuddle up tight. It feels good . . . knowin' that ye . . . you're needed . . . It's the best feelin' . . .

Pax *walks down the aisle and exits.* **Andy** *and* **David** *stand in silence.*

Andy   Davy . . . a mhic . . . he's only . . . huh . . .

David   What . . .?

Andy   Don't mind . . . only his version of . . . his take on the thing. Sure, ye heard him earlier on . . . about Jackie, poisonin' your ear, be Jaysus . . .

David   What . . . what are you . . .?

Andy   About Jackie, ye can't set any store by what . . .

David   Jesus, Andy . . . I'm tryin' to . . . what he's just . . . Fuck, I was there . . . up in the house.

David *starts to move towards the exit.*

Andy   Davy . . . where are ye . . . don't . . . a mhic . . . don't . . .

David *sees the bottle of whiskey and picks it up.*

David   Don't what? Go . . . no, no . . . going to stay . . .
get drunk . . . get absolutely fuckin' pissed, all over again . . .
Come on . . .

He takes a slug of the whiskey, offers it to **Andy**.

David   Come on . . . finish the . . . blind drunk . . . forget
. . . yeah . . . forget and lock up this place, have a great big
cry . . . and go home. Come on . . .

Andy *doesn't move for the bottle.*

David   I was there, ye see . . . one of the Saturdays . . .
up in the house . . .

Andy   Of course ye were, Davy.

David   She was standin' in the kitchen . . . you were
upstairs . . . washing, whatever . . . getting ready for to
bring me home and then come on across here for the night
show. You know, the usual . . .

Andy   Like we always did . . .

David   Only this time I'd asked Marie would she come
with us . . . I said I'd give her two kisses if she'd walk down
the town with us . . . and once I was dropped home she
could come over here and see Omar Sharif. So . . . so it
was all set up . . . she put her coat and scarf on. I put my
hand in hers. You arrived down and you looked at the two
of us . . . Do you remember this . . .? Do you . . .?

Andy   No, Davy . . .

David   You told me to run on ahead, opened the front
door, so I did, and I was waiting at your gate when you
arrived out on your own and I asked where Marie was, and
you said that she'd changed her mind, but I wasn't having
that, ran back and rang the front door, no answer, so I
tapped the window, saw Marie sitting, her coat and scarf off.
She opened the door and said that she wasn't feeling great
and that she'd go next week, that Omar Sharif would wait
for her, and she shut the door again. I . . . I caught up with
you, on the road . . . You must have sensed that I was . . .

pissed off . . . because you explained to me about Marie and
her nerves, as you called them . . . You said that she'd have
to lie down, take her tablets so she'd get well again . . .

Andy   I don't . . . remember.

David   I do, because ye see . . . after that . . . now that
I think of it, after that I was kind of wary around her . . .
didn't chat her up as much . . . didn't take an interest in the
garden with her because I thought she was . . . stayed with
you in the back room . . . away from her. Christ, Andy . . .
Christ . . . what did you . . .? Was this the way you . . .?
You said something to her, didn't ye? Why . . .? Come on,
Andy, take a drink or fuckin' . . .

Andy   Davy . . . she was . . .

David   What . . . she was . . . what . . . your wife . . .
your wife that you . . .

Andy   None of her . . . my wife . . . yeah . . . but none of
her . . . I had my . . . business . . . you were my business . . .
You were such a bright young fella in the house . . . not
hers . . . You . . . you . . . you . . . were there, and I felt . . .
my business . . . felt . . . good . . . that I was kinda lookin'
after ye . . .

David   It was only . . . a few hours on a Saturday.

Andy   It was more than . . . the big empty house across
there . . . At least . . . the chat we had . . . A young fella
like ye needed a chat . . . otherwise that big empty . . .

David   A chat . . . a yarn . . .

Andy   A fuckin' yarn . . . yeah . . . from the films to . . .
to . . . to, ah, we had loads a . . . the other children with ye
in the school . . . like I knew more about them, more in
touch with the local . . . than your da was. The families they
came from . . . So you'd know who to steer clear of . . .
avoid . . .

David   The undesirables . . . the Jimbob Hickeys . . .

Andy   The fuckin' Hickeys . . .

David   I told Dad, when Jimbob first started in on me . . .
I managed to tell him, outside the school as he was dropping
me off, in a hurry, always in a hurry . . . barely looked at
me. Not . . . impressed . . . but told me that all bullies were
cowards and that I was going to have to stand up to him . . .
and I kept this in my head . . . imagining how I'd do it . . .
then I saw the film . . . like Clint . . . that's how I'd do it . . .
like Clint . . . And that's what I told you . . . acting it out,
Jimbob was the Mexican bandido . . . and, 'Then what
happened, Davy?' you'd say. 'And then what did ye . . .'

Andy   I did . . . I did.

David   Big Jimbob sitting on me, rubbing muck in my
face . . .

Andy   But you fought back . . . Punched him in the
stomach, rolled him off ye . . .

David   I stood up to him . . .

Andy   Saw him off . . .

David   That's what I said . . .

Andy   Like Clint would have . . .

David   That's what I said . . . But there was no Clint . . .

Andy   Gave him a fistful . . .

David   There was no Clint . . .

David   I just . . . lay there . . .

Andy   You stood up to him, Davy . . .

David   NO . . . NO . . . NO . . . I . . . Andy, I just lay
there, dirt being pushed into me mouth, tears rolling down
me cheeks and Jimbob sneering at me that I didn't even
have a mammy to go crying home to . . . and every Friday
after that I handed him fifty pence so he'd leave me alone.

Andy   But that's only a . . . ye were only a gassoon . . .
a little white . . . a fib . . .

David But don't you see . . . for years . . . and now . . .
I was going to . . . tonight, another yarn . . . about the
other fella . . .

Andy The other . . .

David The fella . . . the guy that Emma's been carrying
on with . . . Ye see, I was going to . . . She doesn't arrive,
at the end of the night . . . we're locking up and she hasn't
arrived, so that was going to be the story. She'd left me . . .
she'd run off behind my back with this other fella, she was
going to be a spiteful two-faced bitch . . . That was going to
be the yarn . . . do ye . . .

Andy She . . . Davy . . . Is she . . .?

David She's not coming down, she never was.

Andy She's . . . I don't . . . She's gone off . . . with this
fella . . .

David Yes . . . yes, she . . . No, don't ye . . . it doesn't
matter . . .

Andy Jesus, in my head I saw ye's . . . tonight . . . be
Jaysus . . . saw you askin' her up the aisle . . . here . . . a
night never to be forgotten . . .

David Well, that's not going to fucking happen . . .

Andy That other fella's not in the ha'penny place with
you . . . not at all . . . not the end of the . . . can be put
right . . . yeah . . . yeah . . . ah, sure now. Ah, she'll . . .
she's not goin' to . . . I know you . . . You have the way
about ye . . . You'll be well able to sweep her back up off
her, be Jaysus, feet . . . work the oracle with her . . . that's
right, Davy . . .

David Jesus, Andy, there is no other fella. She's not coming
down because . . . because I . . . I don't have that way
about me. Last night . . . fuck . . . her launch last night . . .
biggest night of her life . . . her new band, her music . . . I'm
getting pissed at the bar . . . fucking it all up.

Andy   No, Davy . . .

David   In my stupid addled head it seemed to me that she didn't care, I felt that she was fading away from me, leaving me behind . . . and Jesus, so mad for her, not able to . . . these feelings I . . . have . . . for her . . . Running away from them . . . drinking them away from me . . . shouting and roaring . . . and insulting . . . Had to be thrown out . . . fucked into a taxi but she was still there . . . she was still giving me a chance . . . Call me tomorrow, she said . . . call me when you're ready to talk, really to talk to me, she said. And this morning I picked up the phone in that pub beside busaras, I put the coins in . . . heard her voice . . . heard her say my name, but I just . . . couldn't . . . couldn't . . . hung up . . . couldn't do it, so I ran home here, hoping that there was some kind of . . . something . . .

Andy   You have . . . don't be tormenting yourself . . . a mhic.

David   Where . . . where is the . . .?

Andy   Here, be Jaysus . . . all around ye . . . this place . . . It'll always . . . in your head, be Jaysus . . . live on . . . the walls, the screen, the fuckin' carpets . . . You'll keep that . . . with you . . . the people . . . the . . . us chattin' out there . . . the two of us . . .

David   It's just an empty building . . . it's not . . . there's nothing . . .

Andy   I mean . . . a mhic . . . I mean you still have . . .

David   And that man who didn't bother to ring me tonight . . . and you know he could have . . . could have . . . found a few bob from somewhere . . . but no . . . fucker was too busy selling everything from under me.

Andy   Davy . . . you have . . .

David   Did you see . . . the Penders . . .? They . . . the Penders . . . they have a home . . . Did you hear them . . .? They . . . happy in their . . . feeling of home . . .

Andy   Ah . . . You'll always have a place in this town, up in my house, I told ye that . . . a mhic . . . the end of here but . . . Davy, come here to me . . .

Andy *slowly walks towards* **David** *and awkwardly puts his arms around him.* **David** *stands stock still.*

David   I wanted him . . . for my sake . . . to keep . . .

Andy   I know . . . sssssssh now . . . Davy.

Andy *holds him tighter.*

David   I wanted to laugh with him again.

Andy   I know . . . but he's not here, a mhic . . . He's not here . . . I'm just sayin' it like . . . it's the truth.

David *allows himself to be held. To be comforted.*

David   I just want him to . . .

Andy   A mhic . . .

Andy *disengages from* **David**.

Andy   Listen now . . . the spare room up in the house, waiting for you, be Jaysus, no sense in you bein' on your own over there . . . huh . . . or . . . or I could come over to your house tonight . . . take the drink . . . finish off the wake . . . what do ye say?

David   I . . . no, Andy . . . the wake's over . . .

Andy   Not at all . . . another sup . . . we'll close the doors, we'll lock up . . . go over to yours . . . sit up . . . finish the wake . . .

David   I don't know . . .

Andy *goes to gather up the pile of posters.*

Andy   We can take these across, we can sort through them in your house, because I have one here that . . .

David   What about Marie?

Andy   She'll be all right for one night.

David But don't you always have to ring her . . .? Will she not panic if you don't . . .?

Andy She'll have to survive for one night . . .

David But don't you have to be there to tuck her in . . .?

Andy She'll just have to manage.

David No . . . you couldn't leave her, she'd . . .

Andy Ah, FUCK MARIE . . . fuck her . . . I . . . for years, be Jaysus . . . for one fucking night . . . she can . . . she can GO TO FUCKIN' HELL!

Andy *flings the posters to the floor. They look at each other.*

David Jesus, Andy . . .

Andy I didn't mean . . . it's just the night that's in it . . . has me . . .

David Has you . . . has you . . . fuck . . . what are we . . . WHAT ARE WE . . .?

Andy No, no . . . Davy I . . . I . . . it just came out . . . I do try . . . I do try to do my best . . . I do . . .

David *turns to go.*

Andy I'm sorry . . . forgive me, Davy . . . please . . . If you go . . . I HAVE NO ONE . . .

Andy *goes to grab hold of* **David** *who recoils from his reach.*

David Jesus . . . get away from me . . .

Andy *tries again and grabs hold of* **David**'s *shoulder.*

David Let me go.

David *breaks free of* **Andy's** *grasp.*

David LET ME GO . . .

Andy Ah, Davy . . . don't . . . don't . . . ye don't have to . . . about Marie . . . worry about . . . she'll be grand . . . she'll have taken her sleeping . . . by now . . . pills, do ye see . . . she'll be dead to the world . . . so ye needn't . . .

David   Christ, Andy . . . Why did you . . .? How could
you have let her . . .?

Andy   I . . . a mhic . . .

David   Why did you do that to her . . .?

Andy   I . . . try to . . .

David   Andy . . .

Andy   Try to understand me . . . I . . .

David   Tell me . . .

Andy   I . . .

David   TELL ME . . .

Andy   I WANTED SPARKS . . . I wanted . . . but all
I got was . . . her . . . beside me . . . smilin' at me . . . but
I didn't want . . . I wanted the . . . twinkle . . . you know . . .
you . . . have . . . the twinkle in your . . . you know . . .
you have it . . . Ye see I couldn't . . . I didn't have it to give
to her . . . the . . . warm lovely 'can't live without you'
feelin', you have . . .

David   I have it.

Andy   Do ye see . . . what I'm tryin' to . . . in your . . .
don't let it . . . a mhic . . . don't let it go . . . keep hold of
it. Whatever ye do, try and keep hold of it.

They look at each other, really taking each other in. **David** *eventually
turns to go.*

David   Goodbye, Andy.

Andy *frantically rummages through the pile of posters.*

Andy   Hold on . . . please, Davy . . . come here . . .
lookee here, what I picked out for ye.

He finds the poster he was looking for and opens it out to show
David. *It is a poster for* A Fistful *of Dollars.*

Andy   An original . . . wha' . . . worth it's weight in . . .
there, Davy . . . take that with ye now.

He hands **David** *the poster.*

There's plenty more in the pile, and in the storeroom . . .
tomorrow a mhic . . . think the world of ye, always will . . .
I'll see ye here at eleven . . . in the morning . . . here . . .
in our Savoy . . . right, Davy . . .?

David *does not respond.*

Andy   See ye, then, ye'll be here . . . won't ye . . .?

David *does not respond. He looks down at the poster.*

Andy   Ye will of course . . . Christ I'll never . . . the ol'
chatter of ye, excitement of ye, pointin' up at the posters . . .
but one day ye seemed kinda quiet or upset . . . ah, you
were missin' your ma, and I managed to find a poster for
this Disney yoke called *The Island at the Top of the World*,
'cause I knew that ye had loved it and, be Jaysus, the way
your face lit up, delighted and then . . . badgerin' for to be
brought into the projection box . . . and . . . anyways . . .
I'll see ya tomorrow . . . huh . . .

David *starts to head off towards the exit.*

Andy   Goodnight, a mhic.

Andy *watches him and then adopts cowboy gunfight pose.*

'You see, I understand that you men were just playin''
around, but the mule, he just doesn't get it. Of course if you
were to all apologise . . .' Come on, Davy . . . 'I don't think
it's nice, you laughin', you see my mule don't like you
laughin' . . .' Come on, Clint . . .

David *with some effort joins in, but it is not his usual full-on Clint
impression.*

Andy / David   'Gets the crazy idea that you're laughin' at
him . . . now if you all apologise, like I know you're going
to . . . I might be able to convince him that you really
didn't mean it.'

Andy *flicks his hand out to mime four gun shots.*

Andy   Say it, Davy . . .

David (*complies but again without any gusto*)   'My mistake . . . four coffins.'

Andy (*clapping his hands*)   Deadly . . . 'My mistake . . . four coffins.' Our favourite . . . Goodnight, a mhic . . . see ya tomorrow.

Andy *looks on as* **David** *leaves the auditorium. He waits for a moment before tidying Pax's frames into the tin box. He lifts the piece of floorboard where he had hidden the box and replaces it. He puts the floorboard back. He begins to gather up the posters, but then he notices that David has left the photo of the two of them behind. He picks it up, looks at it and then out into the auditorium.*

Blackout.

Printed in the USA
CPSIA information can be obtained
at www.ICGtesting.com
LVHW020859171024
794056LV00002B/631

9 780413 774408